SpringerBriefs in Population Studies

More information about this series at http://www.springer.com/series/10047

Rok Zupančič · Nina Pejič

Limits to the European Union's Normative Power in a Post-conflict Society

EULEX and Peacebuilding in Kosovo

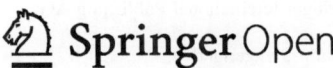

Rok Zupančič
Centre for Southeast European Studies
University of Graz
Graz
Austria

and

Faculty of Social Sciences
University of Ljubljana
Ljubljana
Slovenia

Nina Pejič
Faculty of Social Sciences
Centre of International Relations
University of Ljubljana
Ljubljana
Slovenia

ISSN 2211-3215   ISSN 2211-3223   (electronic)
SpringerBriefs in Population Studies
ISBN 978-3-319-77823-5   ISBN 978-3-319-77824-2   (eBook)
https://doi.org/10.1007/978-3-319-77824-2

Library of Congress Control Number: 2018934919

Printed on acid-free paper

This Springer imprint is published by the registered company Springer International Publishing AG
part of Springer Nature
The registered company address is: Gewerbestrasse 11, 6330 Cham, Switzerland

This monograph was supported by the European Union's Horizon 2020 Programme for Research and Innovation [Grant Agreement No 653371] for the project: "Improving the Effectiveness of Capabilities in EU Conflict Prevention—IECEU" (www.ieceu-project.com), on which both authors worked. The work was also financially supported by the project "The European Union and its Normative Power in a Post-conflict Society: A Case Study of Northern Kosovo—KOSNORTH" [Marie Sklodowska-Curie Individual Fellowship, Grant Agreement No. 655896], led by Dr. Rok Zupančič (September 2016–August 2018).

This monograph was supported by the
European Union' Horizon 2020 Programme
for Research and Innovation (Grant
Agreement No. 653477) for the project
"improving the Health care in Capabilities
in EU Country Preparation—ICU" Fava
[...] an project [...] on which work was
worked. This work was also financially supported by the project "The European Union
and its Normative Power in Risk conflict
Society. A Case Study of Northern Kosovo"
KOSNOR TP, Marie Sklodowska-Curie
Individual Fellowship, Grant Agreement No.
655876) led by Dr. Rok Zupančič
(September 2016–August 2018).

Acknowledgements

This book could not have been published without the project coordinator Kirsi Hyttinen and her team at Laurea University in Finland having put together a team of experienced researchers from across Europe who via hard, good quality collective work sufficiently impressed the EU so that it awarded a EUR 2 million grant for the project "Improving Capabilities in EU Conflict Prevention—IECEU" (Horizon 2020 Programme for Research and Innovation, Grant Agreement No. 653371).

The generous grant allowed the international consortium, including the first author of this book, to develop a robust methodological framework to analyse the EU's civilian missions and military operations in three different regions: Africa, the Middle East and Asia and Southeast Europe (the Balkans). There were two purposes of this comparative analysis: first, to contrast various civilian missions and military operations launched by the EU in underpinning ideas and policy recommendations to help the EU develop a more effective conflict prevention and peacebuilding approach. Second, it led the »academics« within the consortium to strive for theory building within the theories of conflict prevention and peacebuilding. When looking back over the project's 3-year duration, this eternal struggle between the »practitioners« and »academics«, sometimes even sparking loud and fierce discussions, served as an inevitable and inspirational driver of the whole project. (Now, at the end of the project, »the two worlds« no longer seem as far apart as initially appeared.)

Apart from establishing the common analytical approach, this book's authors were primarily responsible for conducting research in »The Balkans« (the formal name of the working package). The main reason the coordinators asked the Slovenian scholars to conduct research in Southeast Europe is that Slovenia was itself a Yugoslav republic up until 1991. It was thus expected the Slovenian researchers' ties with and knowledge of the region are strong. When asked to coordinate the research on »the Balkans«, the book's contributors were particularly pleased since they have both been working *in, on* and *with* this very region for several years. (However, works examining Slovenia's relationship with the Balkans are not always well received by all, especially Slovenia's political leaders who since

1991 and even before formally and informally have been working hard to »de-Balkanise« Slovenia and show the world the country has more in common with Central and Western Europe than with the "problematic" Balkans.)

Apart from the project coordinators, the authors would like to thank the researchers who contributed to the Kosovo section of Working Package 2 of the IECEU project: Ivana Boštjančič Pulko, Nina Čepon and Meliha Muherina (Centre for European Perspective, Slovenia), Johanna Suhonen (Finnish Defence Forces International Centre (FINCENT), Finland) and Blaž Grilj (University of Ljubljana, Faculty of Social Sciences, Slovenia).

Last, but not least, *faleminderit shumë/hvala puno* to Bane Nešović and Florian Qehaja, always willing to help and respond to even our most absurd questions about Kosovo.

Graz, Austria   Rok Zupančič
Ljubljana, Slovenia   Nina Pejič
January 2018

Contents

About the Authors

Rok Zupančič, Ph.D. is a Marie Curie Postdoctoral Fellow at the Centre for Southeast European Studies, University of Graz. Before joining that university, he worked as Assistant Professor at the University of Ljubljana (Faculty of Social Sciences) and was a Principal Investigator in a Horizon2020 project "Improving the Effectiveness of Capabilities in EU Conflict Prevention—IECEU", in which he led a working package on CSDP missions and operations in Southeast Europe.

Nina Pejič is a Ph.D. candidate and Teaching Assistant at the Centre of International Relations at the Faculty of Social Sciences, University of Ljubljana. Before joining the Centre of International Relations, she worked as a Research Fellow at the Centre for Defence Studies, University of Ljubljana, engaged in research as part of the Horizon2020 project "Improving the Effectiveness of Capabilities in the EU Conflict Prevention—IECEU".

Acronyms

CEE	Central and Eastern European
CFSP	Common Foreign and Security Policy
CSDP	Common Security and Defence Policy
EC	European Communities
EDC	European Defence Community
EEAS	European External Action Service
EPC	European Political Cooperation
ESDP	European Security and Defence Policy
EU	European Union
EUHR	European Union High Representative
EULEX	European Union Rule of Law Mission in Kosovo
EUPT	European Union Planning Team
EUSR	European Union Special Representative
FINCENT	Finnish Defence Forces International Centre
FRY	Federal Republic of Yugoslavia
ICITAP	International Criminal Investigative Training Assistance Programme
ICR	International Civilian Representative
IECEU	Improving the Effectiveness of Capabilities in EU Conflict Prevention
IMF	International Monetary Fund
IR	International Relations
KFOR	Kosovo Force
KLA	Kosovo Liberation Army
MMA	Monitoring, Mentoring and Advising
NATO	North Atlantic Treaty Organization
NGO	Nongovernmental Organization
OSCE	Organization for Security and Cooperation in Europe
PID	Programme Implementation Documents
RRM	Rapid Reaction Mechanism

SAP	Stabilisation and Association Process
SFRY	Socialist Federal Republic of Yugoslavia
SRSG	Special Representative of the Secretary-General
UN	United Nations
UNDP	United Nations Development Programme
UNMIK	United Nations Mission in Kosovo
UNPROFOR	United Nations Protection Force
UNSC	United Nations Security Council
UNSG	United Nations Secretary-General
USA	United States of America
USSR	Union of Soviet Socialist Republics
WEU	Western European Union

Chapter 1
Introduction

1.1 The Puzzle

Kosovo is one of the youngest countries in the world. In the last few decades, its history has been turbulent, stained with blood. When the European Union Rule of Law Mission in Kosovo (EULEX) was established back in 2008 as another optimistic effort of the international community to build sustainable peace, Kosovo Albanians, the biggest ethnic group in the country, held high expectations. This is no surprise: Kosovo Albanians have endured difficult periods of violence, particularly during the war of 1998–1999, and despite being citizens of "an independent state" face the challenge of living in one of Europe's poorest countries, dogged by corruption and lawlessness. Although the second biggest ethnic group in Kosovo, the Serbs, does not agree with the Kosovo Albanians on Kosovo's future political status and oppose both its statehood of and international recognition, there is widespread agreement among them: the rule of law in this corner of South East Europe urgently needs to improve.

Professionalising the Kosovar police, customs and judiciary—EULEX's three main working areas—remains an urgent task among a handful of other challenges facing this post-conflict society (economic reconstruction and tackling poverty, for example). The early announcements made by EULEX staff were ambitious: they promised to not only professionalise the key services for democratic society to function properly, but also committed themselves to go after the "big fish" (Qosaj-Mustafa 2010, 5). Unsurprisingly, these promises of bringing the perpetrators to justice made the local population believe sustainable peace and a well-functioning democracy were within reach. Moreover, most Kosovo Albanian political parties supported the deployment of EULEX—with one exception, *Vetëvendosje!* (Movement for Self-Determination), a prominent political party that has been fiercely opposed to EULEX from the very start.

© The Author(s) 2018
R. Zupančič and N. Pejič, *Limits to the European Union's Normative Power in a Post-conflict Society*, SpringerBriefs in Population Studies, https://doi.org/10.1007/978-3-319-77824-2_1

Despite the passing of months and years, only a handful of people have been processed by the courts. Unsurprisingly, the initial euphoria seen in significant parts of Kosovo Albanian society has dwindled. Further, the corruption scandals affecting EULEX itself that resonated widely in post-conflict Kosovo, leading to vigorous reactions of the locals who once believed EULEX could also heal society from other problems—not just those covered by its mandate. More fuel was added to the fire by certain prominent political figures whose political programme included harsh and constant criticism of the international community, especially EULEX.

The Kosovo Albanians' protests against EULEX often turned violent (Krasniqi 2009). One of the biggest protests took place in 2009 when rioters destroyed 28 EULEX vehicles; three police officers and one rioter were wounded. Apart from the protests, the supporters of *Vetevendosje* expressed their outrage with EULEX in different ways on an everyday basis, most notably by writing graffiti describing EULEX as an occupier that should leave the country immediately (McKinna 2013). Yet the Kosovo Serbs were almost equally opposed to the EU's most ambitious civilian mission so far, designed to be a flagship of its Common Security and Defence Policy (CSDP), having argued that the establishment of EULEX *de iure* meant recognition of Kosovo's statehood (Radio Slobodna Evropa 2008).

In a setting where the objectives of EULEX's mandate were very ambitious yet where the mission's approval among the local population has reached its lowest levels in the last couple of years, it is worth investigating why and how this all came about. The lack of an exit strategy and the erosion of its legitimacy are the two main criticisms levelled at the mission (Qehaja and Prezelj 2017, 412–416). It is thus intriguing to explore why the EU—despite EULEX's well-documented disapproval among most residents of Kosovo (both Albanians and Serbs) and the fact this civilian mission is costly yet clearly not delivering on its promises—insists on continuing this rule-of-law mission in this part of Europe.

Conversely, why is the idea of exporting the EU's standards and norms to a third country, which technically speaking is EULEX's overarching aim, so bitterly opposed on the ground? While it is true that Kosovo might be "the laboratory of the international community to test some ideas" (Zupančič 2015), due to its geographical proximity probably it is also the most appropriate space to fulfil the EU's aspirations to finally become recognised as 'a force for good' in international relations—Normative Power Europe (Manners 2002). In line with its attempt to become a global security actor, the EU's normative aspirations extend far beyond Kosovo. Yet, compared to certain other conflict or post-conflict societies where the EU has sought to establish norms (e.g. Southern Sudan, Mali, Chad etc.), Kosovo might—at least *prima facie*—be a relatively easy peacebuilding task. However, as this monograph demonstrates, this has not been the case.

1.2 The Argument in Brief

The EU's peacebuilding role in Kosovo, and the performance of EULEX in particular, have attracted considerable academic criticism in the last few years (Papadimitriou et al. 2007; Shepherd 2009; Kammel 2011; Radin 2014; Malešič and Juvan 2015; Grilj and Zupančič 2016; Qehaja and Prezelj 2017). EULEX has also not been spared of salient criticisms from 'within', when the EU itself launched several investigations to help discover EULEX's malfunctioning as an institution and the misbehaviour of its staff. One case in point is the Jacque Report published in April 2015 in response to accusations of corruption in the judicial sector made by a staff member of EULEX (Jacque 2015). The performance of EULEX and the misconduct occurring under its flag is also strongly rebuked by former staff member Andrea Capussela (2015) who argues in his book that the mission has been so unsuccessful in meeting its objectives that it is better to immediately close it down and withdraw it from Kosovo. It is no surprise that the negative sentiment surrounding EULEX—often rightful, albeit not always—also echoes widely in Kosovar media outlets on an almost daily basis (Kossev 2014; Koha.net 2017).

It is hard to dispute the fact that this, the most ambitious mission ever launched within the CSDP framework, has several problems and as such has not fulfilled the expectations of Kosovo residents themselves (Albanians, Serbs and other ethnic minorities) or the EU politicians and officials overseeing this civilian mission. This book, however, does not attempt to challenge the findings and valid allegations thoroughly researched and documented in the previously mentioned publications. But what this book does challenge is the general belief that EULEX, as part of the EU's peacebuilding project, has done nothing at all and has even played quite a positive role in building sustainable peace in Kosovo.

Thus, the central argument of this book is that certain aspects of EULEX's performance in the 10 years of its operation (2008–2017) *have helped improve* certain practices and further that the mission staff have been learning from their initial mistakes. In particular, this monograph seeks to show the EU is able to project its normative power through its peacebuilding efforts, especially in fields that are *politically unproblematic* and *hence more technical in nature* or—to use military terms—take place on the tactical level (e.g. raising standards of police conduct; improving the customs control; streamlining court procedures).

Yet one must also take into account that the mission has been operating in a very challenging environment since its inception, in both a local and international perspective. One example is the question of the non-recognition of Kosovo by EU member states, which further complicates the EU's effectiveness. It is not even expected that all EU countries will recognise Kosovo's statehood in the near future. If the other structural causes stemming from the complexity of the international community, each significantly impacting the peacebuilding project's success in Kosovo, are added to this conundrum (e.g. the role of the United States of America (USA) in Kosovo and the wider region of South East Europe; the Serbia-Russian Federation nexus and the implications for Kosovo), it would be quite naïve to expect that a single international actor could bring several positive changes to this post-conflict society.

By arguing along these lines and given all the constraints the EU as an institution and EULEX as a 'spin-off' are facing, this book seeks to answer the following *general research objective*: what kind of power is the EU supposed to be (and 'pretends to be') in its peacebuilding endeavours in a post-conflict society in its immediate neighbourhood—the 'new-born' country of Kosovo.

The general research objective is further broken down into several specific *research questions*. First, what are the effects of the EU's attempt to normatively influence the EULEX Kosovo mission? Second, should the EU aspire to be a normative, civilian, transformative, economic or even military power—or perhaps none of these—even though the EU invests "more in development cooperation than the rest of the world combined" (Mogherini 2016, 3)? Third, is it reasonable for the EU to continue to declaratively pursue normative goals on a global scale, attempting "to widen the reach of international norms, regimes and institutions" (European Union 2016, 41), when it even struggles to build sustainable peace in Kosovo, whose around 1.8 million inhabitants represent not even 0.4% of the entire EU population? Finally, what is the direct impact of EULEX's work in its main fields of engagement: the police, customs and the judiciary?

1.3   Methodological Framework

The methodological framework of this monograph is an excerpt of a wider conceptual framework established within the extensive Horizon 2020 project IECEU (Improving Capabilities in EU Conflict Prevention).[1] It draws from an analysis of 66 interviews conducted during field trips to Kosovo and Bosnia and Herzegovina in 2016 within IECEU Working Package 2 (The Balkans). While this monograph focuses on the EU's mission in Kosovo, the data acquired in Bosnia and Herzegovina further shed light on the labyrinths of the CSDP in South East Europe.

The researchers from the University of Ljubljana, the Centre for European Perspective and the Finnish Defence Forces International Centre (FINCENT) interviewed various people from Kosovo (local staff working for EULEX, non-governmental organisations' (NGOs') representatives in Kosovo, and the international staff of EULEX in particular).[2] Some other experts were also interviewed in

---

[1]IECEU 2016. Deliverable 1.4: IECEU Conceptual Framework. Available at: http://www.ieceu-project.com/wp-content/uploads/2016/11/IECEU_Conceptual_Framework_PU.pdf (27 September 2017).

[2]The principal investigator leading the research in South East Europe was Dr Rok Zupančič, University of Ljubljana (Faculty of Social Sciences, Defence Research Centre), now working at the University of Graz (Centre for Southeast European studies). The researchers Ivana Boštjančič Pulko and Nina Čepon from the Centre for European Perspective and Johanna Suhonnen from FINCENT participated in the interviewing in Kosovo.

order to ensure third-party feedback pertaining to EULEX's performance (European External Action Service (EEAS) staff; the representatives of certain armed forces' contingents deployed in the framework of multinational stabilisation forces),was obtained. A semi-structured questionnaire was used for the interviews, providing a suitable means to ensure greater richness and variety in answers, including unexpected ones. The research questions stem from an extensive analysis of academic and expert literature on EULEX and Kosovo in general, which was conducted prior to commencing the field work.

The preliminary findings from the mentioned approach were then critically evaluated at a roundtable discussion. Several experts working in South East Europe or in EU structures were invited to the roundtable in Slovenia in order to assess the findings of the IECEU researchers made during their field work in early 2016. In addition, the representatives of security/enforcement institutions (the Slovenian Armed Forces and the Slovenian Police), the Ministry of the Interior, the Ministry of Foreign Affairs, think tanks and academia participated, with the intention to evaluate the IECEU researchers' findings from as many perspectives as possible. The roundtable discussion had 24 participants and was organised according to the Chatham House rules.[3] The feedback received served as a means for validating and improving the findings of the field work.

1.4   Outline of the Monograph

Chapter 2 presents the methodological framework for studying the EU normative power in post-conflict societies through the lens of peacebuilding. To establish such a framework, it is necessary to understand the EU's aspiration to become a provider of global security since the first modest attempts of the then European Communities (EC) to contribute to international peace; the first section of Chap. 2 analyses this. The second section explores normative power as a theoretical concept and its practical 'embodiment' in the form of EU peacebuilding in post-conflict societies and explains the book's theoretical underpinnings.

Chapter 3 focuses on the EU's involvement as a security actor in South East Europe. It describes the process of the EU gradually recognising the importance of stability in its immediate neighbourhood—a region that was missing an adequate and decisive response from the EU during the 1990s when wars devastated large parts of former Socialist Federal Republic of Yugoslavia (the SFRY, also Yugoslavia)—for EU member states, South East Europe and, finally, also for Kosovo. The second part explores Kosovo's emergence as 'a security problem' from early on in the conflict in Kosovo between the Serbs and Albanians until more recent times, when the (so-called) international community decided to intervene by

---

[3]The list of participants at the roundtable is available in Deliverable D2.4 "Round table—Discussion Report" at http://www.ieceu-project.com/?page_id=197 (9 November 2017).

launching a mission to help build sustainable peace—the very endeavour the EU is today leading.

Chapter 4 first illustrates Kosovo's 'appropriateness' for the EU's peacebuilding efforts, focusing on events that led to the establishment of EULEX. The chapter continues by explaining EULEX's deployment and the scope of its mandate. This is followed by the book's biggest contribution, namely its exploration of best practices, lessons identified and drawbacks in the three fields of EULEX's mandate (police, customs and the judiciary). The analysis is conducted in line with the previously established framework at the nexus of the academic literature on peacebuilding and normative power theory and intertwines three perspectives: the perspective of EU officials in Brussels, that of EULEX staff, and also the locals' perspective on EULEX.

Chapter 5 concludes the monograph. It critically evaluates the research findings and seeks to provide a few theoretical contributions for peacebuilding theories and the theory of the EU as a normative power. It also suggests possible avenues for further research.

References

Capussela, A. L. (2015). *State-building in Kosovo: democracy, corruption and the EU in the Balkans*. London: I.B. Tauris & Co Ltd.

European Union (2016). A global strategy for the European Union's foreign and security policy. Retrieved November 9, 2017, from https://europa.eu/globalstrategy/sites/globalstrategy/files/regions/files/eugs_review_web_0.pdf.

Grilj, B., & Zupančič, R. (2016). Assessing the planning and the implementation of the EU Rule of Law Missions: case study of EULEX Kosovo. *European Perspectives, 8*(2), 63–86.

IECEU (2016). Deliverable 1.4: IECEU conceptual framework. Retrieved September 27, 2017, fromhttp://www.ieceu-project.com/wp-content/uploads/2016/11/IECEU_Conceptual_Framework_PU.pdf.

Jacque, J.P. (2015). *Review of the EULEX Kosovo mission's implementation of the mandate with a particular focus on the handling of the recent allegations*. Report to the attention of the High Representative/Vice President of the European Commission Ms Federica Mogherini. Retrieved January 8, 2017, from http://collections.internetmemory.org/haeu/content/20160313172652/http:/eeas.europa.eu/statements-eeas/docs/150331_jacque-report_en.pdf.

Kammel, A. (2011). Putting ideas into action: EU civilian crisis management in the Western Balkans. *Contemporary Security Policy, 32*(3), 625–643.

Koha.net (2017). Berisha thotë se po hetohet ish-prokurorja e EULEX-it, Marie Bamieh. Retrieved September 27, 2017, from http://www.koha.net/arberi/46317/berisha-thote-se-po-hetohet-ish-prokurorja-e-eulex-it-marie-bamieh/.

Kossev (2014). Koha: Sudije EULEX-a primale mito da zatvore više slučajeva na Kosovu, a tužilac Ratel ometao istrage. Retrieved September 27, 2017, from http://kossev.info/strana/arhiva/korupcija_u_eulex_u/2720.

Krasniqi, E. (2009). *Kosovo: Rethinking EU policy*. Zürich: ETH Zürich.

Malešič, M., & Juvan, J. (2015). Analiza operacij kriznega upravljanja EU. *Teorija in Praksa, 52*(5), 844–864.

Manners, I. (2002). Normative Power Europe: A contradiction in terms? *Journal of Common Market Studies, 2*, 235–258.

McKinna, A. (2013). The Vetevendosje movement in Kosovo: An increasing focus on nationalism. Retrieved September 26, 2017, from http://www.balkanalysis.com/kosovo/2012/02/22/the-vetevendosje-movement-in-kosovo-an-increasing-focus-on-nationalism/.

Mogherini, F. (2016). Foreword to the global strategy for the European union's foreign and security policy. Retrieved September 26, 2017, from https://europa.eu/globalstrategy/sites/globalstrategy/files/regions/files/eugs_review_web_0.pdf.

Papadimitriou, D., Petrov, P., & Greiçevci, L. (2007). To build a state: Europeanization, the EU actorness and state-building in Kosovo. *European Foreign Affairs Review, 12,* 219–238.

Qehaja, F., & Prezelj, I. (2017). Issues of local ownership in Kosovo's security sector. *Southeast European and Black Sea Studies, 17*(3), 403–419.

Qosaj-Mustafa, A. (2010). Strengthening rule of law in Kosovo: The fight against corruption and organized crime. Policy Paper 2010/8. KIPRED: Prishtina. Retrieved September 26, 2017, from http://www.europarl.europa.eu/document/activities/cont/201202/20120201ATT36932/20120201ATT36932EN.pdf.

Radin, A. (2014). Analysis of current events: "Towards the rule of law in Kosovo—EULEX should go". *Nationalities Papers, 42*(2), 181–194.

Radio Slobodna Evropa (2008). Kosovski Srbi protiv EULEX-a. Retrieved September 26, 2017, from https://www.slobodnaevropa.org/a/1293494.html.

Shepherd, A. J. K. (2009). A milestone in the history of the EU: Kosovo and the EU's international role. *International Affairs, 85*(3), 513–530.

Zupančič, R. (2015). *Kosovo: laboratorij preprečevanja oboroženih konfliktov, pokonfliktne obnove in izgradnje države.* Brno: Vaclav Klemm in Plzen: Zapadočeska univerzita v Plzni.

Chapter 2
Assessing Normative Power in Peacebuilding: A Theoretical Framework

2.1 The EU's Path to Becoming a Peacebuilding Actor

The EC—the EU's predecessor—was already evolving as a security actor during the Cold War, mainly with its structural policies aimed at cooperation with developing nations. These policies were introduced as an instrument of long-term peacebuilding in line with the ideological background that economically stable societies are less like to descend into armed conflict (van de Walle 2004). However, despite several attempts to develop supranational security policies—the European Defence Community (EDC) in the 1950s, the Fouchet Plan in 1960—the member states pursued security actions and arrangements separately, not together. Accordingly, security was kept off the common political agenda until the late 1960s when European political cooperation produced a few modest success stories (Gross and Juncos 2011).

Nevertheless, when the period of bipolar confrontation following the Union of Soviet Socialist Republics' (USSR, Soviet Union) dissolution had come to an end, the EC/EU had to face a series of security challenges, with the main ones being in its immediate vicinity (e.g. wars in former SFRY; conflicts in the Middle East; instability in North Africa). The idea the EU could have a stake in building peace around the world emerged as a visible objective of the Union's European Security and Defence Policy (ESDP) and the Common Foreign and Security Policy (CFSP) (Stewart 2006, 12). Therefore, over the last 20 years the EU has transformed from being a product of peace only to a major international security actor that seeks to influence security contexts beyond its borders (Gross and Juncos 2011, 3).

This chapter has three parts. First, it explores the development of peacebuilding as a theoretical concept and considers the conceptualisation of peacebuilding as understood by the EU. Second, the chapter examines the elaboration and formation of the EU's policies and approaches to peacebuilding, in particular which events and motivations impacted EU member states in the process of forming the CFSP and ESDP, or nowadays the CSDP. Finally, the chapter outlines the concept of

© The Author(s) 2018
R. Zupančič and N. Pejič, *Limits to the European Union's Normative Power in a Post-conflict Society*, SpringerBriefs in Population Studies,
https://doi.org/10.1007/978-3-319-77824-2_2

normative power, which is a key theoretical foundation of the book. It does so by exploring the term 'normative power Europe' coined by Manners (2002) and delving further into this theoretical concept.

2.1.1 Conceptualising Peacebuilding

The nature of conflicts in the post-Cold War period is unlike the previous bipolar confrontation of the two major geopolitical blocs. The continued increasing trend of intra-state conflicts after the end of the Cold War and, importantly, the recognition that even intra-state conflicts are to be understood as threats to international peace and security led to international actors' greater ambitions to intervene and prevent violence, therefore accelerating interest in conflict prevention techniques (Stewart 2006, 27–28). In addition, the outcomes of conflicts and the expanded 'scope of peace' in conflict-affected societies attracted ever more attention of actors in the international arena. Other aspects of security (economic, societal, psychological, political, ecological etc.) received more attention from both scholars and policy-makers (Buzan 1991; Grizold 1998).

The central idea behind such perceptions is that "while conflict is normal, violent conflict within and between societies arises from and is sustained by unfortunate attitudes and defective social arrangements" (Morgan 2006). The idea underlying those attitudes and arrangements is not necessarily to be taken as a given, but can be mitigated and corrected. The pioneer of the term "peacebuilding" was Johan Galtung (1976, 297). He similarly argued this can be achieved if peacebuilding actors find structures "that remove causes of wars and offer alternatives to war in situations where wars might occur". Brown (1996) further developed the argument about the underlying causes (structural, political, economic/social and cultural/perceptual) and catalytic factors or proximate causes of conflict (internal and external mass-level factors and external and internal elite-level factors)—addressing them should be the goal of peacebuilding.

The question of when a peacebuilding intervention—comprising the application of several instruments—should begin is vital for scholars in the field. Although usually connected with a post-conflict setting and hence used in the aftermath of a conflict, former United Nations Secretary-General (UNSG) Boutros Boutros-Ghali defined the UN's peacebuilding activities as *preventive* and *post-conflict* in a way that similar or even the same peacebuilding strategies can be applied in different stages of a conflict. In other words, peacebuilding was no longer limited to post-conflict settings but was newly conceptualised to mean a set of similar or the same institutional, economic and social activities introduced to help stabilise a given society (Gross and Juncos 2011).

Peacebuilding is therefore essentially long-term conflict prevention and entails the activities of structural conflict prevention in a conflict-prone setting, pre- or post-conflict. Thus, while the different phases of the conflict circle might require different mechanisms and approaches, they cannot be kept separate as a conflict can move back and forth between stages of the conflict cycle (Duke and Courtier 2009, 4). In other words, a conflict can again escalate and turn violent even though at first sight it seemed the conflict was phasing out.

Over time, different visions, notions and conceptualisations of peacebuilding have evolved. Call (2015, 2–3) notes that initially attention was dedicated to the international monitoring of peace agreements and capacities for their effective implementation. Later on, the focus expanded to reform, monitoring and advising with regard to "political, human rights, electoral, disarmament and demobilisation, humanitarian assistance and policing tasks" (ibid.). Based on analyses of case studies and cross-country comparisons, researchers have tried to identify what exactly is in the basket of activities international actors should be using to be successful peacebuilding actors in a post-conflict society. All this led to the development of theories on peacebuilding (Lambourne and Herro 2008).

Stedman and Rothchild (1996) identify four conditions ("sorts of security") upon which successful peacebuilding relies: military, political, cultural and economic security. Schwarz (2005) argues that peacebuilding actors should address security, welfare and representation in a post-conflict society. Samuels (2006) focuses on constitution-building as a precondition for transforming governance, which should be the basis for peacebuilding. Paris (2004) outlines the failures of liberal peace-building through the democratisation and marketisation processes. Call (2015, 3) suggests that peacebuilding actors should move away from "large international-footprint peacebuilding" since some of these early notions of the concept proved to be "short-sighted, overly optimistic, insufficiently nuanced and unrepresentative of global perspectives". Reychler (2004) connects sustainable peace with the notion of peacebuilding and refers to the absence of physical violence, elimination of discrimination, high levels of legitimacy and the ability to constructively transform a conflict.

Some peacebuilding failures in the 1990s were followed by criticism of the liberal design of peacebuilding; the so-called top-down approach in peacebuilding that chiefly emerged early on in the theory's development could no longer satisfactorily explain the complexity of the current developments in post-conflict areas (Leonardsson and Rudd 2015; Qehaja 2017). Critics argued that research attention should be refocused to move away from big and influential international actors to, for example, 'ordinary people'. Authors like Pickering (2007); Mac Ginty (2010) and Paffenholz (2010) wanted to know how these 'ordinary people' build the micro-foundations of peace and to examine their role as peacebuilding actors in these processes.

The discussion within this approach has two central dimensions of the 'local turn in peacebuilding'. The first refers to the local in peacebuilding as a way of enhancing effectiveness. It emphasises local ownership and local capacity-building, as well as local governance models as pillars of peacebuilding (Menkhaus 2006; Bland 2007; Klem and Frerks 2008; Hayman 2010; Siegle and O'Mahony 2010; Björkdahl and Gusic 2013). The second dimension orients to the local as a means of emancipating the 'voices from below' and argues for the inclusion of local agency in peacebuilding analyses (Lundy and McGovern 2008; Autesserre 2010; Paffenholz 2010; Mac Ginty 2010; Richmond 2013; Qehaja 2017).

Some ideas have proven valuable in the long term. This led several international actors to ensure their institutional development regarding peacebuilding also incorporated these ideas by encompassing 'traditional knowledge', built on the experiences of international organisations in the field, states' interests, bureaucratic tendencies, and resource limitations (Call 2015, 3). These 'good practices' are multi-faceted and include a commitment to establishing military, legal, political, economic, social, cultural and psychosocial conditions in a post-conflict society able to promote a culture of peace. They seem to be transformative in terms of changing the relations into sustainable partnerships. Thus, some authors (Lederach 2000; Pugh 2000; Stover and Weinstein 2004; Barnes 2006) contend that such actions should be contextual, meaning they take particular cultural and conflict contexts into account and that local civil society's participation and representation in the peacebuilding processes is vital. Hence, in theory the current prevailing view is there is a need for 'a transdisciplinary mind-set' that encompasses lessons and insights from many perspectives (multidimensionality and inter-disciplinarity) and creates a more contextual, inclusive and holistic peacebuilding theory, with practical applicability (Lambourne and Herro 2008).

However, as Barnett et al. (2007, 53) point out, the problem of the concept's multidimensionality is that while all peacebuilding actors might support the idea of building peace, "they will operate with considerable differences of interpretation regarding the meaning and practice of peacebuilding", since they will all adopt a meaning, activities and policies of peacebuilding that is consistent with their interests, worldviews and mandates. This may suggest that all international peacebuilding cooperation is inherently political and that different peacebuilding actors will act according to various strategies for achieving durable peace in a given post-conflict society that are not necessarily solely based on 'best practices' arising from experience. This indicates peacebuilding could ultimately be a political accomplishment that "might be settled by bureaucratic and political power" (Barnett et al. 2007, 54). Moreover, the lack of a clear definition of the concept or accompanying strategy could produce an outcome which "can be challenged by efficiency, coordination and sustainability issues" (Duke and Courtier 2009, 4).

2.1.2 The EU's Understanding of Peacebuilding

Growing interest in the conceptualisation of peacebuilding in 'EU terms' emerged in European studies alongside the EU's institutional and policy development (Gross and Juncos 2011, 3). As Natorski (2011, 2) argues, this was not part of any pre-conceived general policy. The approach of the EU to peacebuilding instead emerged in response to events in the international community and general international discussions on peacebuilding. Later on, the EU adopted a mixed set of white papers, strategic documents and guidelines that were gradually translated and incorporated into its activities.

Gross and Juncos (2011) note that even EU officials have no clear picture of what peacebuilding actually entails. Further, the various EU institutions (agencies, directorates, EU delegations in foreign countries etc.) do not always agree on understanding of the term. In the Commission's vocabulary, peacebuilding is an instrument for preventing conflict. The latter generally refers to both long-term and short-term measures, including not only rapid preventive reactions to conflicts on the verge of erupting, but also preventing further escalation of current conflicts, including post-conflict stabilisation. As an activity covering all stages occurring before and after the start of conflict, it may be applied to all phases of a conflict, including in peace (ibid.).

Yet the Council uses different wording. In its perspective, peacebuilding forms part of crisis management and thus includes state-building, confidence-building and monitoring activities during the post-conflict stabilisation phase. There is hence a real possibility of the Commission and the Council's instruments overlapping each other in the post-conflict stabilisation phase. Nonetheless, in practice developments have gradually blurred the distinction between the definitions within the EU framework (ibid.).

The current EU approach to peacebuilding therefore entails numerous strategies, practices and instruments. The EU toolbox includes the CSDP missions which serve as a more operational face of peacebuilding as opposed to the structural side (development cooperation, humanitarian aid, improvement of trade policies and other areas in the Commission's domain).[1] These are the 'Council's prerogative' and include both civilian peacebuilding (civilian crisis management) and military crisis management (military operations).[2]

In the context of CSDP missions, the EU also relies on the instruments of disarmament, demobilisation, post-conflict monitoring and security sector reform. the expanded toolbox in the missions includes "tackling trans-regional and cross-border threats such as terrorism, illegal immigration, trafficking of drugs and arms, human trafficking, piracy, security aspects of climate change and governance of natural resources in the conflict" (Natorski 2011, 2).

In addition, the EU often introduces peacebuilding instruments not normally associated with peacebuilding, like state governance reforms (reconstruction of state institutions and economic reforms) and reforms of the judiciary (EUNPACK 2016).

---

[1]The Directorate-General for International Cooperation and Development (DG DEVCO) is responsible for creating EU development policy on post-conflict countries and managing external aid to cover specific needs of a country during a transitional post-conflict period. Through external aid, DG DEVCO also formulates policies focused on reducing poverty, sustainable economic, social and environmental development, promoting democracy, the rule of law, good governance and human rights (EUNPACK 2016, 18).

[2]The terminology is unclear in the EU documents; although it is only in recent years that peacebuilding has been effectively mentioned in the documents, these instruments qualify as peacebuilding according to our aforementioned definitions.

It is also noted that "/O/n the strategic level there has been a shift from a focus on the concept of deep democracy—political reform, elections, institution building, anti-corruption, independent judiciary and support to civil society as promoted by the EU High Representative (EUHR) Catherine Ashton—towards a more pragmatic approach focusing on stabilisation and support of state-building, with less emphasis on the democratic elements of governance, as set in the EU's Global Strategy launched in June 2016 and promoted by the EUHR Frederica Mogherini" (EUNPACK 2016, 17).

Another tool available to the EU is preventive diplomacy. The EU has been partaking in negotiations on several peace agreements or ceasefires (such as in the Indonesian province of Aceh and South Sudan) and various kinds of reconciliation processes (such as the dialogue between the governments of Serbia and Kosovo). Hence, mediation instruments form part of the EU's pre- and post-conflict response. This is managed by the bodies tasked with preventing conflict or post-conflict response, such as the EU Special Representative (EUSR) that works as a negotiator of peace agreements and ceasefires on the EU's behalf and tries to contribute to the overall stability of an affected region. Examples here include the Horn of Africa, Kosovo, Bosnia and Herzegovina, Georgia, Afghanistan (European Union External Action 2016).

2.2 The EU's Development as a Security Actor

2.2.1 From Conceiving the 'Peace Project' Onwards

If we look at the actual practice of peacebuilding and conflict prevention (implementation), we immediately become aware that in its essence the European integration is a massive peacebuilding and conflict prevention project built on the ashes of the World War II. When the six founding European countries (Belgium, Netherlands, Italy, Luxembourg, West Germany and France) signed the Treaty Establishing the European Coal and Steel Community in 1951 and so established the EC, this marked the start of European integration efforts. This process per se reflects the goal of peacebuilding as the EC was established to make another war in Europe unlikely (Gross and Juncos 2011, 3).

The EC's origins and early and consistent commitment to matters of peace historically characterise the EU's responses in the field of security. At the time, the peacebuilding dimension of the EC rested on the premises of economic integration, supported by political reasoning. This directly corresponds with attempts by the Copenhagen School of security studies to expand the concept of security from military to other domains (Buzan 1991). However, the motivations to effectively combine security and economic objectives have been consistent and kept pace with the geographical expansion of the EU. Over the years, they have evolved into institutional structures, norms, rules and standards aimed at promoting action in the security field (Kirchner 2006, 951).

The idea of the EDC seen in the Pleven Plan[3] proposed in the 1950s was the first attempt to form a pan-European defence force. It was meant to provide an alternative to North Atlantic Treaty Organization (NATO) membership for European countries. Yet the EU decided to remain a 'civilian power' (Kirchner 2006, 951–2). This was due to two 'French' objections: first, the French Parliament refused to ratify the documents required for its creation and, second, then French President Charles De Gaulle was opposed any kind of further supranational integration and insisted that the security of countries in the EC remain in the hands of NATO and the Western EU (WEU) (Stewart 2006, 44).

In the 1950s and 1960s, the member states therefore tried to give the internal market a foreign policy aspect, but failed. However, in the late 1960s the French political environment saw a big change. In 1969, the then President Charles De Gaulle resigned. His successor, President Georges Jean Raymond Pompidou, saw a return to support for the supranational political ideas; thus, further integration of the European continent was again a viable option for the Community. This idea is also reflected in the Luxemburg Report,[4] which led to the establishment of European Political Cooperation (EPC) in 1970. This helped enhance regular intra-governmental contacts and improve dialogue among foreign ministries of EC member states (Zupančič 2016, 17–18).

In the early 1970s, this foreign policy cooperation among the member states started to attract world attention: the Community began to develop an international voice, formed through quiet, long-term preventive diplomacy. However, the Community's economic and political activities that had provided for the security dimension in its external relations also gained a treaty basis in the Single European Act of 1986.[5] Conflict prevention in non-military ways therefore fell within the scope of the treaty and soon became one of the EC's vital activities, representing a small yet important step towards a common approach to its external relations. Nevertheless, as emphasised, the explicit strategy for preventing armed conflict still rested on the "export of the virtuous circle of political and economic stability to its closest neighbours" (Zupančič 2016, 19).

---

[3]René Pleven was the French Prime Minister between July 1950—March 1951 and August 1951—January 1952. The plan was proposed in October 1950 by Pleven and drafted mainly by Jean Monnet. The EDC was to include West Germany, France, Italy, Belgium, the Netherlands and Luxemburg (Guillen 1993, 131).

[4]The Luxemburg or Davignon Report (1970) was drafted subsequently after the summit in The Hague in 1969, in which EC heads of states instructed their ministers to "study the best way of achieving progress in the matter of political unification, within the context of enlargement" (Communiqué of the meeting of Heads of State or Government of the Member States at The Hague, 1969). The report created informal governmental consultation mechanisms (Ginsberg 1989).

[5]Single European Act (1986). Amending the Treaty Establishing the European Economic Community of 1957, signed on 17 February, entered into force 1 July 1987.

The EU's approach to conflict prevention in this period was thus expressed in a range of policies containing either direct or indirect mandates (Kirchner 2006, 954). The EC took advantage of this on several occasions, aiming to secure peace in countries were aspiring to join the union (for example in Greece in 1982, or Spain and Portugal in 1986). In the accession process for Central and Eastern Europe (CEE), the European Commission used a 'carrot and stick approach' to decrease tensions in interstate disputes. Two cases of the EC's activities to prevent conflict help understand its preventive approach to interstate tensions that might otherwise have turned into a serious interstate conflict.

The first case is the dispute between Hungary and then Czechoslovakia over construction of the Gabcikovo-Nagymaros hydroelectric project on the Danube in the late 1980s.[6] For some time, the EC remained an observer of the conflict and had offered that its ministers of environment technically assess the project. It was only in the 1990s when the EC duly recognised that the dispute is of a political and not a technical nature, thereby changing its initial perspective, admitting the conflict was a sensitive and tricky problem that was political in nature. As a result, the EC became involved as a mediator (Fürst 2003), although its success here was mixed. Although the conflict never became violent, which might otherwise have happened "had the countries not felt the decisive diplomatic pressure 'from Europe'" (Zupančič 2016, 19), no long-term solutions could be found. The compromise agreement brokered in 1993 was not observed by Slovakia and the case was submitted to the International Court of Justice.

The second example may be described as the successful conflict resolution by the EC is the case of Estonia in which the Russian-speaking minority 'found itself' living after the Soviet Union's dissolution and Estonia's declaration of independence. The international community strongly pressured Estonia to resolve the status of the Russian-speaking minority. The Estonian government was pressured by the EU to provide equal citizenship rights for the Russian-speaking minority, the same as those enjoyed by ethnic Estonians (Kronenberger and Wouters 2004). The EC's approach was efficient since it was non-asymmetric in character (an influential supranational power backed by the strongest EU countries *versus* a feeble country that had just stepped out on the path of independence).

The lesson drawn from these cases is that the EC's first attempts in the area of conflict prevention activities were explicitly structural in character, meaning they involved a wider perspective and greater scope of targets and actions in the longer

---

[6]This is a largest barrage project on the Danube, initiated by the two socialist countries under the Budapest Treaty of 1977. It was aimed at preventing floods, improving the Danube's navigability and producing clean electricity (emission-free water power seemed to be the right opportunity for the production of energy in the high air pollution region of northern Hungary and Czechoslovakia). However, due to economic hardship, Hungary tried to abandon the project in 1981 and two years later the two countries agreed to slow down the works. In 1989 Hungary completely abandoned the works due to public pressure and waves of protests. As a result, Czechoslovakia decided to implement part of the scenario, as well as river diversion, extracting 90% of the water from the riverbed. Consequently, water levels dropped 2 m, triggering an international conflict (Fürst 2003, 2–3).

term, as opposed to operational conflict prevention, which "aims at giving an immediate answer to an imminent crisis" (Melander and Pigache 2007, 13). This structural approach focused on the mechanisms then available to the EC, such as targeted trade policies and conditionality of development aid. Several African, Caribbean and Pacific states benefited from this structural approach (ibid.).

Though these activities, the EC learned that if it wants to play a role in conflict prevention, for example as a mediator, it needs to have credible sources of power (political, economic, military, normative etc.) that can be levered to mitigate a dispute (Zupančič 2016, 20–22). However, the EU gave no systematic emphasis to multi-faceted conflict prevention that would include operational (direct) conflict prevention. The reason for this is that the Cold War environment had disabled (or at least caused the reluctance of) 'other' international actors to interfere in the sphere of influence of either superpower, the USA or the USSR. Another reason is the EC was preoccupied with its own horizontal and vertical development and had no ambitions or capability to become an international security actor.

2.2.2 The Post-Cold War Period

The end of the Cold War and the new geopolitical context created new challenges for the European continent, especially in terms of security. A series of events and occurrences led to this: the international community was destabilised after the so-called Eastern bloc fell apart, the SFRY broke up, bringing violent conflicts (in Croatia, Bosnia and Herzegovina, and Macedonia during 1992–1995, and then in Kosovo in 1998–1999), devastating conflicts were still underway in the Middle East and Asia while, importantly, there was a lack of appropriate structures and mechanisms for dealing with conflict prevention and conflict resolution at the regional and international level.

The EC soon became aware of these changes and started to adopt measures to address the new challenges. Its political and security structures had to adapt to the new-look environment in which the security paradigm had changed. A few solutions and ways forward were proposed by scholars who called for newly emerging aspects of security to be included in understanding of the security paradigm; besides military security, namely the core of Cold-War understanding of security, economic, political, societal, psychological and ecological security appeared on the agenda as vital concepts pertaining to security (Buzan 1991).

Since the EC was at that time internally relatively safe, member states turned their ambitions to the idea of institution developing into a credible actor in international relations, or even 'a force for good' (Manners 2002). The UNSG also acknowledged the importance of conflict prevention and stated that it must become a new norm of international relations. Hence, the focus shifted from the previous focus on national security to a 'culture of prevention', which became a buzzword in international organisations (Zupančič 2015)—all of a sudden, several institutions wanted conflict prevention to be one of their main *raison d'êtres*. The EC also captured the *zeitgeist*. Apart from the EC's influence in the European periphery, there was a mismatch between its internal political relevance and ability to act politically in the outside world. As Mark Eyskens, the Belgian Foreign Minister, stated in 1991 "Europe is an economic giant, a political dwarf and a military worm" (quoted in Eckhard 2016, 88). In an effort to redress this situation, the EC elaborated its own concept of conflict prevention, which became perceived as not merely preventing imminent crises but as an approach that should lead to long-term and sustainable peace. The EC started to follow an integrative approach to its policies based on the better integration and inter-agency coordination of the existing foreign, security and defence policies (ibid.).

The ambition for the European project to further move into the realm of security and contribute to maintaining world peace also found a basis in the Treaty on the EU (Maastricht Treaty signed in 1992 and entering into force in 1993). This document is treated as a milestone in the European integration process. In essence, the Treaty brought EPC Cooperation into the institutional framework of the (newly named) EU. The renamed CFSP was now included in one of the three pillars of the EU's structure. Unlike EPC, the scope of the reformed institution was more comprehensive and also covered the objective to preserve peace and strengthen international security.

According to the Treaty, the CSFP was meant to help ensure the EU's more active external efforts in creating a more favourable international environment that enabled it to improve its capacity in anticipating the outbreak of crises and tackle problems at their roots. The regions of focus were prioritised in the Treaty: CEE, the Commonwealth of Independent States, the Balkans, the Mediterranean, and the Middle East. With respect to the new situations in CEE after the Cold War, the encouragement of the prevention and settlement of conflicts was noted as an objective, although in the context of the Organization for Security and Cooperation in Europe (OSCE).

Yet there is no direct reference to the term conflict prevention in the Treaty, even though the issues identified were clearly relevant for conflict prevention (Wouters and Naert 2004, 4–5). The WEU was seen as particularly important to the Union back then, before the Treaty of Amsterdam was introduced and the ESDP along with it. In its Petersberg Declaration (1992), the WEU declared its willingness to support the conflict-prevention activities of the Conference on Security and Cooperation in Europe and the UN on a case-by-case basis. With this, the EU acquired the possibility to request support for conflict-prevention activities from the WEU, bringing defence implications. Although not so many conflict-prevention measures appear to hold direct implications for defence issues, it provided strong support for the EC/EU's path towards launching the ESDP in the late 1990s (Wouters and Naert 2004, 6).

As mentioned, one region identified as an EU priority was the Balkans, but it soon became clear the EU was then incapable of dealing with a crisis on its doorstep (the violent dissolution of the SFRY). Therefore, it became necessary for the EU to further develop its capabilities, allowing it to try to prevent conflict before it happens. Some early attempts at creating a more systematic approach were put in place (Wouters and Naert 2004, 24–25).[7]

The war in Kosovo between the armed forces of the Federal Republic of Yugoslavia (FRY) and the Kosovo Liberation Army (KLA), in the years of 1998–1999 ravaging in the EU's immediate vicinity coupled with the EU's impotence to intervene triggered increased efforts in the field of conflict prevention that coincided with the ESDP's development. The ESDP was a policy with a strict intergovernmental character, established by the European Council Declaration on Strengthening the Common European Policy on Security and Defence, as annexed to the conclusions of the Cologne European Council of 1999 (ibid.).

The stalemate ended in 2001 when the EU Programme for the Prevention of Violent Conflicts was adopted by the European Council in Gothenburg. This strategic document set conflict prevention as one of the objectives of the Union's external relations (Council of the EU 2001). Also in 2001, the Commission issued a Communication on Conflict Prevention that reaffirmed development cooperation is one of the instruments available to the EU to address the root causes of conflicts, in line with the theory of conflict prevention (Rummel 2004, 14).

A series of concrete actions followed these political commitments. In 2001, the Rapid Reaction Mechanism (RRM) was established. As Zupančič (2016, 24) notes: "this was also an attempt of the EU to address various criticism of being too reactive and less proactive as a conflict prevention actor in global affairs". This mechanism enabled the EU to respond more rapidly to urgent situations. It also offered a reasonable degree of autonomy to the Commission, albeit limited by the member states. The RRM's role was to take over operations lasting up to six months. It had an annual budget of some EUR 30 million. Around 50 projects in 25 countries were streamlined through the mechanism, but it struggled due to several constraints. Lavallée (2012), for example, mentions the RRM's inability to ensure the coordination of activities that fell between a short-term crisis response and long-term development assistance.

Therefore, the EU was both "a pioneer of and a latecomer in conflict prevention" (Rummel 2004, 1). This means that the EU as such is an ambitious project, aimed at establishing peace on the continent through cooperation among European nations. But at the same time the evolution of its conflict-prevention activities lagged behind other EU policies in the fields of trade, monetary integration, environment, law etc. The fact the EU was a leading actor in certain other dimensions made its weak record in managing conflicts and establishing peaceful zones outside its borders seems all the more astounding (ibid.). Thus, it is not surprising that policies such as the CFSP made their way up the priority list of EU member states by way of a remedy to the abovementioned shortcomings.

---

[7]For example, the European Parliament planned to establish the EU Analysis Centre for Active Crisis Prevention. However, the attempt failed. A policy planning and early warning unit was set up by the Council of the EU, tasked with providing assessment and early warning of situations that would have implications for the EU's foreign and security policy. The Commission also funded a Conflict Prevention Network in 1997 (Wouters and Naert 2004, 24).

With the RRM in place, the EU soon adopted the European Security Strategy, acknowledging the debate on the external threats facing the EU and committing itself to using the instruments developed to prevent armed conflicts (European Security Strategy 2003). New threats, such as terrorism, weapons of mass destruction, organised crime or state failure were identified and linked to the 'traditional' problems of regional conflicts. The Strategy also paid great attention to the notion of development, naming security as a precondition for it. Multilateral diplomacy was advocated as a means to work together with other actors engaged in conflict prevention. Importantly, the need to assist failing and failed states and a regional approach to peacebuilding were clearly emphasised (Zupančič 2016, 24).

In 2007, the Commission reorganised its assistance and cooperation programmes and proposed the Instrument for Stability. This instrument was a substantial improvement over the RRM. The EU obtained better control over the budget, the limitation of the provisions concerning the definition of short and long-term conflict prevention was improved, and projects became more flexible in duration. With this, the EU's comprehensive approach to conflict prevention, as well as to peacebuilding, was reinforced (Zupančič 2016, 25).

2.2.3   After the Treaty of Lisbon

The next institutional change regarding the EU's conflict prevention came with the Treaty of Lisbon in 2009.[8] The legacy of the WEU was incorporated in the Treaty as part of the so-called Petersberg tasks. Further, the policy of conflict prevention became an integral part of the CSDP and thereby contextualised with permanent structural cooperation. Importantly, the Lisbon Treaty clearly outlined the structures responsible for implementing conflict prevention in practice: the President of the European Council together with the EUHR for CFSP became chiefly responsible for it.

Established to assist the EUHR, the EEAS is significant in conflict prevention for the connectivity it establishes between the different bodies dealing with conflict prevention in the Commission and the Secretariat of the Council. Another benefit of the EEAS is that it is staffed with experts from all member states. As Duke mentioned in 2001 (quoted in Zupančič 2016, 26), "increased the synergies among the EU's external instruments, moving further towards a strongly integrated approach in crisis response and conflict prevention". Moreover, the two competitive departments of the Council and the Commission, the Situation Centre and the Crisis Room, were included in the EEAS to increase its coherence. From a practical viewpoint, this is an important improvement in terms of the operability of the structures for conflict prevention: daily contacts among stakeholders became more frequent and coordinated since they were physically present in the same building (Lavallée 2012).

In the last few years, the EU has been affected and challenged more than ever by geopolitical changes, conflicts, insecurity and instability often due to or exacerbated

---

[8]The Lisbon Treaty, signed 13 December 2007 in Lisbon, in force since 1 December 2009.

by the lack of effective and accountable security systems (European Commission 2017). The growing potential for individuals to create large security threats and transnational criminality has further complicated the EU security landscape (European Commission 2015). Especially the ongoing crises in its vicinity, "from the conflict in Ukraine, to the rise of Islamic State and the refugee situation in the Global South, have made the improvement of external response capacities a top priority" (EUNPACK 2016). Hence, the European Agenda on Security 2015 emphasises that external conflict and insecurity, especially when originating in the EU's immediate neighbourhood, sometimes associated with radicalisation and violent extremism, also affect the EU's internal security.[9] In addition, the new Global Strategy offers a new way to foster the EU's peacebuilding capabilities through an integrated approach (EU Global Strategy 2016, 9).

2.2.4   Future Challenges to EU Conflict Prevention and Peacebuilding

Ensuring a sufficiently capable EU is a precondition for it to operate as a security actor—the EU must first guarantee its own security and second be able to assist or take the lead role in stabilisation processes around the world. Ever since the Lisbon Treaty, the EU has been improving its internal coordination and focusing its efforts on restructuring its approach. The current challenges faced by the EU are likely to continue in the future, but the member states' defence budgets have been severely cut in the last few years. This hampers the EU's ability to develop, deploy and sustain its military capabilities. The need for the EU's external actions to become more effective, visible and to increase their impact was recognised and emphasised at a meeting of heads of states. The European Council firmly committed itself further the development of a "credible and effective CSDP" and make "the efficiency and effectiveness of the EU Comprehensive Approach, including as it applies to EU crisis management" a priority (European Council 2013).

The EU's transformation as an international actor able to influence conflicts abroad through its military, especially its civilian, presence represents a new kind of power in international politics (Diez and Manners 2007). The EU itself has dealt with difficulties in conceptualising its 'identity' throughout these developments. The construction of its identity holds important implications: on one hand, it is a precondition for other actors to agree with the norms promoted by the EU and, on the other, it defines the relationship between the EU and the image of 'others' (ibid.).[10]

---

[9]The European Agenda on Security, Commission's Communication to the European Parliament, the Council, the European Economic and Social Committee and the Committee of the Regions 2015.

[10]In this way, the EU as a normative power "constructs a particular self of the EU (and it is perhaps the only form of identity the diverse set of actors within the EU can agree on), while it attempts to change others though the spread of particular norms" (Diez and Manners 2007).

It remains an unsettled question of what type of power the EU is endowed with. Almost half a century ago, Duchêne (1973, 43) called it "civilian power". Hedley Bull's (1982) criticism of the concept followed, together with and Hill's (1990) inquiry into whether the EC is a political or civilian power.[11] With the hasty and ambitious development of the CFSP, Manners (2002) introduced "Normative Power Europe" into the academic debate. The concept moved from theory to policy discussions when 'adopted' as part of the official discourse by EU actors themselves.[12] This is not surprising since normative power is not so intrusive in character and as such is more acceptable for constructing the EU's identity in international politics. Further, it is also more likely to find acceptance among the member states, than more intrusive or interventionist comprehensions of power projection. Diez and Pace (2007, 2) note that "the EU actors see themselves (and the EU as a whole) as a 'force for good' in conflict situations, and indeed in world politics generally speaking". The EU is therefore not only discussed, but also perceives itself, as a normative power (Forsberg 2011, 1186).

2.3   The EU's Struggle for Normative Power in Post-Conflict Societies

By analysing the state-of-art in the field of normative power from 2002 on, when the concept was introduced to the theory of International Relations (IR), the overarching goal of this chapter is to develop the argument that the EU uses the instruments of peacebuilding—construed as meaning what it considers appropriate or inappropriate action—as a way of building its image as a normative actor.

2.3.1   Power in International Relations

In the field of IR, power has long been considered the main concept of realism. Morgenthau (1960, 5) stated it is a human desire to dominate, think and act in line with our interests, which are defined as 'power', whereas power is the ultimate goal of all states. Since then, the concept of power has been used to make theoretical sense of state behaviour in international politics. Weber defined power as the ability

---

[11]Hill (1990) argued the EC could not be a civilian power since it can use coercive instruments.

[12]Diez and Pace (2007) note the concept of self-representation as a normative power and a 'force for good' is especially common in the Commission and the Parliament, but also not a stranger to the Council. The Commission is defending the principle more forcefully than others as a guardian of the integration and associations processes (that can be part of the broader peacebuilding politico-strategic objective). Moreover, Forsberg (2011) mentions the key EU representatives, such as Commission President Barroso, have endorsed the concept of 'normative power Europe'.

to have one's will prevail (within a social relationship) despite resistance or opposition (Weber 1976, 28).

It does not matter what this opportunity (to prevail) is based on; Dahl similarly defines power as "A getting B to do something B would otherwise not do" (Berenskoetter 2007). Yet, there is a second dimension of power which lies in the 'non-decision', the ability to prevent a certain decision from taking place. For example, this second dimension can be considered while analysing security problems in institutions, such as agenda-setting: political leaders of states discuss, define and decide on security problems and seek appropriate responses to them (ibid.).

The third dimension of power is the power to shape normality. This is still a developing concept in IR, which has gained the attention of scholars with Nye's (1990) suggestion that 'soft power' underpinned the USA's successful leadership in the post-Cold War period. The third dimension is an analysis of the influence of culture, language, ideas, identities, norms, values etc.—'soft' and 'normative' power terminology thereby entered the IR vocabulary (Berenskoetter 2007). It soon became the key vehicle for explaining the influence of Germany, Japan, EC or Association of Southeast Asian Nations countries and institutions with the presumed contributions to the 'global good' (Zupančič and Hribernik 2013). Any debate on normative power cannot overlook Manners' definition (2002) of normative power, namely "an ability to shape conceptions of 'normal' in international relations" (Manners 2002).

Most definitions of power tend to distinguish different types of power: economic power, military power, soft power, hard power, smart power, power over opinion etc.[13] Although this distinction of power-types mainly serves analytical purposes, this way of comprehending power may unintentionally blur one of the core assumptions made in this paper: that the understanding of a normative power agency cannot be separated from the question of what normative power agents means for projecting normative power (spreading norms in the international community).

2.3.2 Understanding Normative Power: What Is It (not)?

How does normative power differ from other types or comprehensions of power? If it is relatively easy to describe what hard power is (coerciveness or force to influence the behaviour and actions of another actor), one may rightly argue that the distinction between normative power and soft power is unclear. At a basic level, the latter is defined as the ability to attract others so that they start wanting what you want. In other words, it is the ability to obtain what you want through attraction rather than coercion or payment. Soft power, as acknowledged in Nye's later works, should be understood as an empirical (positive/descriptive) more than a theoretical

---

[13]See, for example: Carr (1962); Nye (1990); Manners (2002).

concept (Nye 2004; Rothman 2011). Based on this definition, soft power is a foreign policy tool while normative power is an explicitly theoretical concept requiring an understanding of social diffusion and normative practices (Diez and Mannes 2007).

We follow the logic proposed by Diez and Manners (ibid.). They argue that soft, civilian and normative power are all closely related because a civilian power actor, relying on soft power, advocates and practises particular kinds of norms—above all, the use of civilian means to achieve their policy goals. Therefore, civilian power can be perceived as a specific form of normative power. From the above theoretical insights, we may conclude that normative power does not imply a logic of exclusiveness. On the contrary, it can sit alongside other forms and sources of power (military, economic, cultural etc.) since certain actors in international relations realise that building up their normative power capacities can complement other forms of their power, including military, if used in the pursuit of normative goals, thereby positively impacting their image in international relations.

Another question concerning normative power is whose norms and which particular ones matter: which international actor has the power to advocate and spread norms around the globe, and thus to persuade other countries to adopt the advocated norms (or at least to ensure 'target countries' adopt them). Norm-spreading has a stronger impact if it is encouraged by an influential international actor (Zupančič and Hribernik 2013). At that point, one might wonder if the norm itself, without being supported by instruments of hard power, can succeed.[14] Björkdahl (2007) adds to understanding of norms/normative powers by arguing that the construction and promotion of norms is a strategy for setting international normative standards and thereby influencing the world order. Kavalski (2013) elaborated the concept when arguing that normative power is not necessarily about affecting other actors' perceptions, but mostly about framing their responses.

The latter argument is important for the methodology followed by this book since it presupposes that 'a force for good' should also be recognised and accepted as 'a force for good' by others. However, as Tocci (2008)[15] warns, along with other authors, e.g. Sjursen (2006) and Staeger (2016), analysts should be careful not to engage in some imperialistic imposition of norms by judging what is subjectively considered as 'good' on the grounds of presumed universality. Thus, the concept of normative power tends to rest on the assumption there are cosmopolitan norms and values that transcend the particularistic claims of discrete political communities (Zupančič and Hribernik 2013).

Some authors believe the claims that an international actor is 'a normative power actor' contains a hegemonic notion vis-à-vis others because one particular subject of international relations (a country, international organisation, or others) may claim

---

[14]For more insights on whose norms matter, see Acharya, A. (2004). How Ideas Spread: Whose Norms Matter? Norm Localization and Institutional Change in Asian Regionalism. *International Organization*, 58(2): 239–275.

[15]Also see: Abasova, M. (2012). 'Normative Power Europe' in Conflict Transformation: A case study of the Israeli-Palestinian conflict. Linköping: Linköping University.

it knows how to cure the diseases of others, or define what is good and declare that definition shall apply to the world as a whole (Zupančič 2011). This understanding resonates with Janusch (2016) who suggests a way to escape the hidden trap of the supposedly imperialistic conceptualisation of (European) normative power by proposing it instead be scrutinised by the logic underlying its acts rather than looking at it through the lens of the questionable universality of the diffused norms.

Tocci's (2008) distinction between normative and imperial powers is premised on whether their agency is 'others-empowering' or 'self-empowering'. In addition, Manners (2002, 242) defended his original argument, noting that "the EU's normative difference comes from its historical context, hybrid policy and political-legal constitution" and that the main force for its policy comes from transnational and supranational organisations reflecting a combination of norms from civil society and European political elites. In other words, the EU's own normative constitution inclines Europe to act in a normative way.

But how can an international actor make use of its normative power and become 'a force for good'? Several authors have proposed different methodological contributions with the aim to analyse ('measure') normative power. Manners' (2002, 242) original idea was to suggest six ways that norms can be diffused (contagion, informational diffusion, procedural diffusion, transference diffusion, overt diffusion and cultural filters), which are relevant for subsequent attempts to analyse normative power. Some insights also emerge from analytical frameworks preceding Manners' paper for measuring political impact, for example Ginsberg's model (2001). Manners (2008) made a further contribution with his debate on tripartite-framework, which draws on ethics to structure a framework according to which the EU's normative power can be analysed in terms of three categories: principles, action and impact.

Forsberg's contribution (2011) is important from a methodological viewpoint as it introduces the concept of an ideal-type normative power actor, namely one towards which real-life actors can only aspire.[16] Namely, an actor can never be an absolute normative power, but can only approach it. He comes to this conclusion based on analysis of a five-part definition that seeks to grasp the core of normative power, thereby answering the question of 'what constitutes normative power" or how does an actor become a 'force for good'. His five-part definition requires a normative power to have 'a normative identity', 'behave according to norms', 'use normative means of power', 'pursues normative interests', and 'achieve normative ends'.

---

[16]Also see: Sinkkonen, V. (2013). *The Reactions of the European Union and the United States to the January 25th, 2011 Revolution in Egypt: A Comparative Appraisal of Normative Power*. MA Thesis. Turku: University of Turku.

2.3.3 Analysing Normative Power in Peacebuilding: A Methodological Framework

Forsberg (2011) uses Manners' argument that the EU is a normative power because it possesses a normative identity. Yet Manners uses this as an objective more than a subjective term; he bases the EU's normative identity on conditions, such as hybrid polity and treaty-based order. Next, he argues it is plausible that the EU sees itself as a representative of normative power and because several other actors in world politics might also perceive it as holding normative power. However, it is not self-evident that a hybrid polity with its own legal order cannot use military force or behave in a non-normative way. Moreover, the EU has already started to construct a military dimension, which has not changed the two factors on which Manners places its foundations for normative power (hybrid polity and treaty-based legal order). In addition, the EU's hybrid character is an outcome of a 'Westphalian brake' through which the member states have been resisting supranational developments—and not a symbol of "post-modern values that are internalized in Europe and the EU being a peace project" (Forsberg 2011, 1192).

The same applies to the concept of peacebuilding which also does not originate in the EU having a treaty-based legal order since it evolved without a legal 'constitutional' basis in the treaties (and was only institutionalised with the Lisbon Treaty). In addition, the hybrid order seen in the division of responsibilities between the EC/the EU and the Council is a consequence of the 'Westphalian brake' rather than a success attributable to the values of peace since the EU had a greater chance to influence positive developments through the creation of the EDC.

Consequently, we will analyse normative identity as a subjective term, therefore the identity constructed by the EU and via its interactions with others, which is in line with Forsberg (2011). EU officials feel obliged to contribute to peace and throughout the years the EU has also institutionally built its image as a security and peacebuilding actor. The EU can therefore also be perceived as a self-proclaimed normative power holder in the area of peacebuilding, following the general popularisation of peacebuilding that started at the end of the Cold War. Due to the image of it being a leading actor in certain dimensions, the EU's weak record in managing conflicts and establishing peaceful zones beyond its borders seems disappointing. Thus, the EU has had to keep pace in this field as well, while not possessing significant military capabilities for this purpose.

Next, a normative power should have normative interests, assuming these interests are not, as Tocci (2008) puts it, "self-empowering" but "others-empowering". Toje (2008) argues the EU's normative interests distinguish this institution from other international actors since it has the will to participate in foreign policy dimensions that are a statement of values (not necessarily means- or ends-oriented). Hence the EU—in its attempts to become a normative actor in peacebuilding— should first establish the normative goals it wants to achieve (for example, the organisation of democratic elections, improvement of the human rights situation etc.), which should be perceived as a 'force for good' (the interests should be consistent with the peacebuilding goals).

Third, in line with the normative power theory, a normative actor should behave according to the norms it sets. Forsberg (2011) agrees that the EU mostly abides by international law. However, when considering its endorsement of the NATO military campaign against the FRY in 1999, which had no UN Security Council (UNSC) approval, this becomes questionable (without the support of several EU member states, the military campaign would have been very difficult to conduct). Forsberg (ibid.) mentions other examples of the EU breaking international trade rules and placing its treaty-based laws ahead of international humanitarian law.[17] The methodological viewpoint adopted by this monograph is therefore that an actor (the EU) should maintain its presumed normative power character (by acting consistently with the norms and principles) in its peacebuilding strategy.

Fourth, a normative power should use normative means of power, not for example military or economic means. It should realise its existing obligations, persuade by referring to the general rules and practices and to future mutual gains enabled by possible cooperation. It should also live up to previously made (legal) commitments. In our analysis of the EU's peacebuilding activities, we will apply these presuppositions through the lens of the EU's operational and structural activities and instruments. The latter refer to development cooperation, humanitarian aid etc. and are mainly an expression of economic power.

The EU has tried to broaden the security concept from military to other domains (conflict prevention and peacebuilding also rest on the premises of economic integration, political reasoning, the 'carrot and stick approach' and the promise of becoming a member state). Through its operational activities the EU engages in civilian peacebuilding consisting of monitoring, law enforcement training, and enhancing capabilities of the judiciary etc.—with the aim of supporting activities that uphold so-called European practices or values, such as fair elections, an independent rule of law, a strong civil society, or an anti-corruption mentality. Overall, the EU should foster long-term peace in post-conflict societies by using peacebuilding instruments enhanced by the power of normativity, an issue we aim to investigate.

Finally, an actor should achieve normative ends that should also be a 'force for good'. These normative ends have already been shown to be mixed and contested in the EU. Some good examples are provided by Manners (2002), such as the abolition of capital punishment. Moreover, the EU has functioned as a 'force for good' in ecology, or by signing the Kyoto and Paris climate agreements. However, there are still only a few examples of real success stories (Forsberg 2011). Our interpretation of this point with regard to the concept of peacebuilding is the normative end of a peacebuilding actor should be to 'correct' and adapt the attitudes and

---

[17]See, for example, the judgements *Kadi v. Council of the European Union and Commission of the European Communities.* (2008). Court of Justice of the European Union, 3 September *and Hungary vs. Slovak Republic.* 2012. Court of Justice of the European Union, 16 October.

behaviour that led to the violent conflict, including by addressing the underlying causes and creating the means to resolve the conflict without violence by offering successful alternatives to the scenario of war, and also to prevent triggers of the conflict from intensifying.

These points are crucial for understanding the link between the 'normative power argument' and peacebuilding. Presenting a normative actor as a Weberian 'ideal type' means an actor (the EU) could strive to become and thus be perceived a normative actor. Yet to some extent it is also allowed to fail; it can be more or less successful in its endeavours. Therefore, the key problem of interest is the extent to which the EU can be described a normative actor in the peacebuilding field: are the EU's peacebuilding activities and interests in peacebuilding normative in character; is the EU using "others-empowering means" and providing a meaning of them consistent with the EU's worldviews and values? This monograph will focus on one aspect of both normative and peacebuilding theory through the EU's peacebuilding activities in Kosovo—specifically the EULEX Kosovo civilian mission as a peacebuilding instrument. The normativity of the EU's actions will be analysed in three areas of EULEX's engagement: police, customs, and the judiciary.

References

Abasova, M. (2012). 'Normative Power Europe' in conflict transformation: A case study of the Israeli-Palestinian conflict. Linköping: Linköping University.
Acharya, A. (2004). How ideas spread: Whose norms matter? Norm localization and institutional change in Asian regionalism. International Organization, 58(2), 239–275.
Autesserre, S. (2010). The trouble with the Congo: Local violence and the failure of international peacebuilding. Cambridge: Cambridge University Press.
Barnes C. (2006). Governments & civil society organisations: Issues in working together towards peace. Discussion paper for GPPAC Strategy Meeting in The Hague in October. Retrieved January 8, 2017, from http://www.cries.org/filemanager/fileuser/25.pdf.
Barnett, M., Kim, H., O'Donnel, M., & Sitea, L. (2007). Peacebuilding: What is in a name? Global Governance: A Review of Multilateralism and International Organisations, 13(1), 35–58.
Berenskoetter, F. (2007). Thinking about power. In F. Berenskoetter & M. J. Williams (Eds.), Power in world politics. London: Routledge.
Björkdahl, A. (2007). Swedish norm entrepreneurship in the UN. International Peacekeeping, 14 (4), 538–552.
Björkdahl, A., & Gusic, I. (2013). The divided city—a space for frictional peacebuilding. Peacebuilding, 1(3), 317–333.
Bland, G. (2007). Decentralization, local governance and conflict mitigation in Latin America. In D. W. Brinkerhoff (Ed.), Governance in post-conflict societies: Rebuilding fragile states (pp. 207–225). Abingdon: Routledge.
Brown, M. E. (1996). The international dimensions of internal conflicts. Cambridge: MIT Press.
Bull, H. (1982). Civilian power Europe: A contradiction in terms? Journal of Cutaneous Medicine and Surgery: Incorporating Medical and Surgical Dermatology, 12(2), 149–164.
Buzan, B. (1991). People, states, and fear: An agenda for international security studies in the post-cold war era. Boulder, CO: Lynne Rienner.
Call, C. (2015). The evolution of peacebuilding: Improved ideas and institutions? Tokyo: United Nations University Centre for Policy Research.

Diez, T., & Manners, I. (2007). Reflecting on normative-power Europe. In F. Berenskoetter & M. J. Williams (Eds.), *Power in world politics* (pp. 173–188). New York: Routledge.

Diez, T., & Pace M. (2007). Normative power Europe and conflict transformation. Paper for presentation at the 2007 EUSA Conference, Montreal, 17–19 May. Retrieved September 20, 2017, from http://aei.pitt.edu/7798/1/diez-t-01a.pdf.

Duchêne, F. (1973). The EC and the uncertainties of interdependence. In M. Kohnstamm & W. Hager (Eds.), *A nation writ large? Foreign policy problems before the EC.* London: Macmillan.

Duke, S., & Courtier A. (2009). EU peacebuilding: Concepts, players and instruments. Centre for the Law of the EU External Relations Working Paper. Retrieved July 31, 2017, from http://www.asser.nl/upload/documents/11172009_41811clee09-3comb.pdf.

Eckhard, S. (2016). *International assistance to police reform: Managing peacebuilding.* London: Palgrave Macmillan.

EU Global Strategy. (2016). Shared vision, common action: A stronger Europe. Brussels: High Representative of the Union for Foreign Affairs and Security Policy/Vice-President of the European Commission. Retrieved September 20, 2017, from https://eeas.europa.eu/top_stories/pdf/eugs_review_web.pdf.

EUNPACK. (2016). Understanding the EU's crisis response toolbox and decision-making processes. Deliverable 4.1. Retrieved September 18, 2017, from http://www.eunpack.eu/sites/default/files/deliverables/Deliverable%204.1.pdf.

European Agenda on Security. (2015). Commission's Communication to the European Parliament, the Council, the European Economic and Social Committee and the Committee of the Regions, 2015.

European Commission. (2015). Joint Communication to the European Parliament and the Council: Capacity building in support of security and development—enabling partners to prevent and manage crises. Retrieved July 30, 2017, from http://eur-lex.europa.eu/legal-content/EN/TXT/PDF/?uri=CELEX:52015JC0017&from=EN.

European Commission (2017). Security and development, conflict prevention and the comprehensive approach. Retrieved July 30, 2017, from http://ec.europa.eu/europeaid/policies/fragility-and-crisis-management/links-between-security-and-development_en.

European Council (2013). Conclusions of the European Council (19/20 December 213). Retrieved July 30, 2017, from http://data.consilium.europa.eu/doc/document/ST-217-2013-INIT/en/pdf.

European Security Strategy (2003). Adopted by European Council on 12 September 2013, Brussels. Retrieved July 30, 2017, from http://www.consilium.europa.eu/uedocs/cmsupload/78367.pdf.

European Union External Action (2016). EU special representatives. Retrieved September 5, 2017, from https://eeas.europa.eu/headquarters/headquarters-homepage_en/3606/EU%20Special%20Representatives.

Forsberg, T. (2011). Normative power Europe, once again: A conceptual analysis of an ideal type. *Journal of Common Market Studies, 49*(6), 1183–1204.

Fürst, H. (2003). The Hungarian-Slovakian conflict over the Gabcikovo-Nagymaros dams: An analysis. *Intermarium, 6*(2).

Galtung, J. (1976). Three approaches to peace: Peacekeeping, peacemaking, and peacebuilding. In J. Galtung (Ed.), *Peace, war and defense: Essays in peace research* (Vol. II, pp. 297–298). Copenhagen: Christian Ejlers.

Ginsberg, R. H. (1989). *Foreign policy actions of the EC: The politics of scale.* Boulder: Lynne Rienner.

Ginsberg, R. H. (2001). *The European Union in international politics: Baptism by fire.* Lanham: Rowman & Littlefield Publishers Inc.

Ginty, R. (2010). Hybrid peace: The interaction between top-down and bottom-up peace. *Security Dialogue, 41*(4), 391–412.

Grizold, A. (1998). *Međunarodna sigurnost: Teorijsko-institucionalni okvir.* Zagreb: Fakultet političkih znanosti.

Gross, E., & Juncos, A. E. (2011). *Making sense of EU conflict prevention and crisis management: Institutions, policies and roles.* London: Routledge.

Guillen, P. (1993). France and the defence of Western Europe: From Brussels Pact (March 1948) to the Pleven Plan (October 1950). In N. Wigershaus, & R.G. Foerster (Eds.), *Western security community: Common problems and conflicting interests during the foundation phase of the North Atlantic Alliance.* Oxford: Berg.

Hayman, C. (2010). Ripples into waves: Locally led peacebuilding on a national scale. Peace Direct and the Quaker United Nations Office. Retrieved September 20, 2017, from http://www.peacedirect.org/wp-content/uploads/Ripples-into-Waves-PeaceDirect-concept-paper.pdf.

Hill, C. (1990). European foreign policy: Power bloc, civilian model—or flop? In R. Reinhardt (Ed.), *The evolution of an international actor. Western Europe's new assertiveness.* Boulder: Westview.

Janusch, H. (2016). Normative power and the logic of arguing: Rationalization of weakness or relinquishment of strength. *Cooperation and Conflict, 51*(4), 504–521.

Kadi v. Council of the European Union and Commission of the European Communities. (2008). Court of Justice of the European Union, 3 Sept. Joined cases C-402/05 P and C-415/05 P. Retrieved January 8, 2018, from http://eur-lex.europa.eu/legal-content/EN/TXT/?uri=CELEX%3A62005CJ0402.

Kavalski, E. (2013). The struggle for recognition of normative powers: Normative power Europe and normative power China in context. *Cooperation and Conflict, 48*(2), 247–267.

Kirchner, E. J. (2006). The challenge of European Union security governance. *Journal of Common Market Studies, 44*(5), 947–968.

Klem, M., & Frerks, G. (2008). How local governments contribute to peacebuilding. In A. Musch, C. van der Kalk, A. Sizoo, & K. Tajbakhsh (Eds.), *City diplomacy* (pp. 47–74). Hague: VNG International.

Lambourne, W., & Herro, A. (2008). Peacebuilding theory and the United Nations Peacebuilding Commission: Implications for non-UN interventions. *Global Change, Peace & Security, 20*(3), 275–289.

Lavallée, C. (2012). From the Rapid Reaction Mechanism to the Instrument for Stability: The empowerment of the European Commission in crisis response and conflict prevention. *Journal of Contemporary European Research, 9*(3).

Lederach, J. P. (2000). Journey from resolution to transformative peacebuilding. In C. Sampson & J. P. Lederach (Eds.), *From the ground up: Mennonite contributions to international peacebuilding* (pp. 45–55). Oxford: Oxford University Press.

Leonardsson, H., & Rudd, G. (2015). The 'local turn' in peacebuilding: A literature review of effective and emancipatory local peacebuilding. *Third World Quarterly, 36*(5), 825–839.

Lisbon Treaty, signed 13 December 2007 in Lisbon, in force since 1 December 2009. Retrieved January 8, 2018, from http://www.europarl.europa.eu/ftu/pdf/en/FTU_1.1.5.pdf.

Lundy, P., & McGovern, M. (2008). Whose justice? Rethinking transitional justice from the bottom up. *Journal of Law and Society, 35*(2), 265–292.

Manners, I. (2002). Normative power Europe: A contradiction in terms? *Journal of Common Market Studies, 2*, 235–258.

Melander, E., & Pigache, C. (2007). Conflict prevention: Concepts and challenges. In W. Feichtinger & P. Jureković (Eds.), *Konfliktprävention zwischen Anspruch und Wirklichkeit.* Wien: Austrian National Defence Academy.

Menkhaus, K. (2006). Governance without government in Somalia: Spoilers, state-building, and the politics of coping. *International Security, 31*(3), 74–106.

Morgan, P. M. (2006). *International security: Problems and solutions.* Washington: CQ Press.

Morgenthau, H. J. (1960). *Politics among nations: The struggle for power and peace.* New York: McGraw Hill.

Natorski, M. (2011). The European Union peacebuilding approach: Governance and practices of the Instrument for Stability. PRIF-Report no. 111. Frankfurt: Peace Research Institute Frankfurt. Retrieved September 21, 2017, from https://www.hsfk.de/fileadmin/HSFK/hsfk_downloads/prif111.pdf.

Nye, J. (1990). Soft power. *Foreign Policy, 80,* 153–171.

Nye, J. (2004). *Soft power: The means to success in world politics.* New York: PublicAffairs.

Paffenholz, T. (2010). *Civil society and peacebuilding: A critical assessment.* Boulder, CO: Lynne Reinner.

Paris, R. (2004). *At war's end: Building peace after civil conflict.* Cambridge: Cambridge University Press.

Pickering, P. M. (2007). *Peacebuilding in the Balkans: The view from the ground floor.* Ithaca, NY: Cornell University Press.

Pugh, M. (2000). *The social–civil dimension in regeneration of war-torn societies.* London: Macmillan Press.

Qehaja, F. (2017). *International or local ownership? Security sector development in post-independent Kosovo.* Washington D.C.: Westphalia Press.

Reychler, L. (2004). Peace architecture: The prevention of violence. In A. H. Eagly, R. M. Baron, & H. V. Lee (Eds.), *The social psychology of group identity and social conflict* (pp. 133–146). Washington, DC: American Psychological Association.

Richmond, O. P. (2013). Failed statebuilding versus peace formation. *Cooperation and Conflict, 48,* 378–400.

Rothman, S. B. (2011). Revising the soft power concept: What are the means and mechanisms of soft power? *Journal of Political Power, 4*(1), 49–64.

Rummel, R. (2004). The EU's involvement in conflict prevention—strategy and practice. In J. Wouters & V. Kronenberger (Eds.), *Conflict prevention: Is the European Union ready?.* Brussels: TMC Asser Press.

Samuels, K. (2006). Post-conflict peace-building and constitution-making. *Chicago Journal of International Law, 6*(2).

Schwarz, R. (2005). Post-conflict peacebuilding: The challenges of security, welfare and representation. *Security Dialogue, 36*(4), 429–446.

Siegle, J., & O'Mahony, P. (2010). Decentralization and internal conflict. In E. Connerley, K. Eaton, & P. Smoke (Eds.), *Making decentralization work: Democracy, development, and security* (pp. 135–166). Boulder, CO: Lynne Rienner.

Single European Act. (1986). Amending the Treaty Establishing the European Economic Community of 1957, signed 17 February, entered into force 1 July 1987.

Sinkkonen, V. (2013). *The reactions of the European Union and the United States to the January 25th, 2011 Revolution in Egypt: A comparative appraisal of normative power.* MA Thesis, University of Turku, Turku.

Sjursen, H. (2006). The EU as a 'normative power': How can this be? *Journal of European Public Policy, 13*(2), 235–251.

Staeger, U. (2016). Africa–EU relations and normative power Europe: A decolonial pan-African Critique. *Journal of Common Market Studies, 54*(4), 981–998.

Stedman, S. J., & Rothchild, D. (1996). Peace operations: From short-term to long-term commitment. *International Peacekeeping, 3*(2), 17–35.

Stewart, E. J. (2006). *The European Union and conflict prevention: Policy evolution and outcome.* Berlin: Lit.

Stover, E., & Weinstein, H. M. (2004). Conclusion: A common objective, a universe of alternatives. In E. Stover & H. M. Weinstein (Eds.), *My neighbor, my enemy: Justice and community in the aftermath of mass atrocity* (pp. 323–342). Cambridge: Cambridge University Press.

Tocci, N. (2008). *Who is a normative foreign policy actor? The European Union and its Global Partners.* Brussels: Centre for European Policy Studies.

Toje, A. (2008). The consensus-expectations gap: Explaining Europe's ineffective foreign policy. *Security Dialogue, 39*(1), 121–141.

van de Walle, N. (2004). The economic correlates of state failure: Taxes, foreign aid, and policies. In R. I. Rotberg (Ed.), *When states fail: Causes and consequences.* Princeton University Press: Princeton.

Weber, M. (1976). *The agrarian sociology of ancient civilizations.* London: New Left Books.

Wouters, J., & Naert, F. (2004). The EU and conflict prevention: A brief historic overview. In V. Kronenberger & J. Wouters (Eds.), *The European Union and conflict prevention: Policy and legal aspects*. Haag: Asser.

Zupančič, R. (2011). Normative power as a means of a small state in international relations: The role of Slovenia within 'the EU concert' of normative power in the Western Balkans. *Lithuanian Foreign Policy Review, 25,* 56–76.

Zupančič, R. (2015). *Kosovo: Laboratorij preprečevanja oboroženih konfliktov, pokonfliktne obnove in izgradnje države*. Brno: Vaclav Klemm in Plzen: Zapadočeska univerzita v Plzni.

Zupančič, R. (2016). The European Union and the (r)evolution of its strategy of conflict prevention. *European Perspectives, 8*(2), 16–38.

Zupančič, R., & Hribernik, M. (2013). Normative power Japan: The European Union's ideational successor or another "contradiction in terms"? *Romanian Journal of Political Science, 13*(2), 106–136.

Chapter 3
The EU's Affair with Kosovo

In the 1990s, as part of efforts to build a new, post-Cold War identity the EU made a significant endeavour to become seriously involved in the successful management and resolution of conflicts in its close vicinity (Keukeleire and MacNaughtan 2008, 242). The turbulent region of South East Europe, and the so-called Western Balkans within it, thus seemed to be an appropriate testing ground for 'testing' the power and credibility of the EU.[1] Several studies had focused on the EU's efforts to stop war in former Yugoslav countries, showing the EU had reacted poorly to the outbreak of those conflicts (Andreatta 1997; Joseph 2005; Juncos 2005; Keukeleire and MacNaughtan 2008). As Wouters and Naert (2004, 9) point out, "the EU undertook numerous, but mostly rather unsuccessful diplomatic efforts to prevent, contain and resolve the conflict". After the failure of the EU to preserve or establish peace in its neighbourhood in the 1990s, the countries of the Western Balkans remained a site for the EU to further develop and improve its capabilities, with the goal of integrating the region into the European family and stabilising it in the process.[2]

The EU's interaction with the former Yugoslav countries has had a major impact on how the EU's foreign policy has developed, particularly the CSDP.[3] The main question explored in this chapter is how and why the EU became involved in the armed conflicts in former Yugoslavia or, better, how and why did the EU 'drag' itself into these conflicts? Further, how did the notion of peacebuilding develop in the Western Balkans region in the 1990s and what did the EU learn from these interventions? Why did the EU later become involved in the conflict in Kosovo so voraciously; alternatively, when and why did it start to think that Kosovo might provide a way for the EU to show it is developing into a global security actor with

---

[1]Croatia, Bosnia and Herzegovina, Serbia, Montenegro, Macedonia and Albania.

[2]As mentioned in Chap. 2 with regard to the institutional development of these capabilities, "with the end of the 1990s, the war in Kosovo in the EU's vicinity and at the same time, impotence of the EU to intervene, this increased action in the field of conflict prevention coincided with the development of the ESDP".

[3]For more, see Chap. 2.

© The Author(s) 2018
R. Zupančič and N. Pejič, *Limits to the European Union's Normative Power in a Post-conflict Society*, SpringerBriefs in Population Studies,
https://doi.org/10.1007/978-3-319-77824-2_3

both the means and willingness to act decisively for the sake of international and regional peace?

The next chapter aims to give insights into the EU's gradual recognition of the importance of this region being stable, the history of the Kosovo conflict and how it was managed prior to the EU's full-scale involvement.

3.1   Engaging the EU in "The Blood-Stained Balkans"

> To those who have not visited them, the Balkans are a shadow-land of mystery; to those who know them, they become even more mysterious... You become, in a sense, a part of the spell, and of the mystery and glamour of the whole. You contract the habit of crouching over your morning coffee in the café and, when you meet a man of your acquaintance, at least half of what you say is whispered, portentously. Intrigue, plotting, mystery, high courage, and daring deeds—the things that are the soul of true romance are today the soul of the Balkans. (Todorova 2001, 14)

The Balkans has historically been perceived not only as politically enigmatic and complex—somewhat Delphic—but in derogatory terms, at odds with European values and traditions (Juncos 2005): barbaric, uncivilised, prone to violence and lagging behind "the developed" (Zupančič and Arbeiter 2016).[4] Such discourse on the Balkans and other similar "Balkanisms" (Todorova 2001)—not to mention the wars in the 1990s—have not done much good for the region.

Yet, taking into account the politico-economic reality in the former Yugoslavia until the war in the 1990s, the EC actively engaged with the country mainly through contractual trade relations. It actually became the SFRY's most important foreign market, taking up as much as 60% of the country's exports. The EC did not perceive the SFRY as either the East or the West; its relationship with SFRY was much more extensive than the relation with any other CEE state during the Cold War. Ginsberg (2001, 59) names this relationship as a "history of firsts" in East-West relations.

The SFRY was the first CEE state to accredit its diplomatic representative to the Commission and open a diplomatic mission in Brussels already in 1968. It was also the first CEE country to negotiate and implement a formal trade agreement with the EC in 1970. The EC opened its mission in Belgrade in 1980. The EC's trade and diplomatic relations with Belgrade were founded on the Community's concept of *ostpolitik*—the opening and normalisation of relations with the Eastern bloc, especially by the Federal Republic of Germany (West Germany)—with the CEE states. On the other hand, the former SFRY was a major beneficiary of the EC's Generalised System of Preferences, a system of reduced tariffs on imports of goods from developing countries (ibid.).

---

[4]Derogatory terms "such as the term Balkanization, were already in use following the Ottoman Empire's demise at the turn of the 20th century, when Serbia, Montenegro, Greece, Romania and Bulgaria achieved statehood" (Zupančič and Arbeiter 2016).

In the 1970s, the SFRY was placed within the framework of the EC's new Mediterranean Policy that linked the Community's tariff preferences and economic assistance to states and thereby helped the EC to promote peace and stability in volatile regions. The EC and the SFRY signed another preferential trade accord in 1973 in which each signatory offered the other most-favoured-nation treatment. By 1989, the two had already entered a new Cooperation Agreement that further extended the scope of their bilateral cooperation (Ginsberg 2001, 59–60).

In this post-Tito period, the EC made arrangements to help stabilise the country, and initiated improvements in the cooperation accord etc. In this regard, Ginsberg (1989, 124) claims these improved relations were designed to send signals to the USSR regarding the EC's interests in the country's territorial integrity and political sovereignty; the indivisibility of the SFRY was also strongly favoured by the USA (Zupančič 2016). Moreover, by the end of 1980s the EC and the former SFRY had decided to include meetings at the political level in their cooperation, reflecting the position taken by both sides that it was necessary to cement their relations amid the big changes happening in the CEE states and the Soviet Union. Yugoslavia also asked for new loans in 1989. Yet just as relations between the EC and the SFRY were developing in this new political framework of cooperation, the SFRY came to the verge of unravelling (Ginsberg 2001, 59–60).

Before the wars in the former SFRY during the 1990s, the country's former political elites presented its "socialist society" to the world as an ideal form of multicultural coexistence. In 1980 and after the death of the Yugoslav leader Josip Broz—Tito, who had managed to keep a lid on different alleged and actual inter-ethnic tensions, fuelled by a desire to form independent political entities the various nations in the SFRY started to more decisively pull the national(istic) strings in the direction of creating independent republics (Juncos 2005). These desires were also driven by the geopolitical changes brought by the end of the Cold War.

It is also crucial to understand the economic factors underpinning the complexity of former Yugoslavia. One should note that when the Partisans emerged victorious from the World War II, they were confronted with a very difficult economic legacy—this was especially obvious in the periphery of the country since the SFRY was very unevenly developed. An urgent measure undertaken by the Yugoslav government to counter this was to decentralise the country, which later inspired the separatist tensions of individual republics and autonomous regions—decentralisation led to growing income differences between the richest republics and poorest regions. The gap between the per capita social product of Kosovo and the richest republic, Slovenia, expanded from 1:4 to 1:7 between 1952 and the late 1980s (Becker 2017, 841–842). Kosovo's per capita social product amounted to a mere 30% of the Yugoslav average at the time, while Slovenia's level was up to 200% (Rusinow 2008, 260).

In the 1980s, when the country was hit by a significant economic crisis, the republics and regions were characterised by the heavy proliferation of decentralised social, educational and cultural institutions, as well as strong patterns of uneven economic development.[5] Becker (2017, 841) notes "this crisis had its roots in the attempt to bridge the chronic account deficit and to modernise the economy through capital goods imports, which incurred external debt in the 1970s". The government reacted by applying austerity programmes in the 1980s that were controlled by the International Monetary Fund (IMF), but these led to economic stagnation, a decline in GDP, inflation, increasing poverty and rising unemployment (Becker 2017, 842).

Again, the impact of this crisis hit Yugoslavia unevenly. Djeković (1989, 25) noted that unemployment in Kosovo was 30% while Slovenia had almost full employment with an unemployment rate not exceeding 2%. Together with the clear outbreak of nationalism, which often occurred at the expense of other nations, these circumstances only contributed to the SFRY falling apart (Daskalovski 2003). At the end, this resulted in more than 100,000 deaths, 2.4 million refugees and more than 2 million additional people who were internally displaced (Watkins 2003, 10).

During the wars in the 1990s, several foreign journalists reproduced and recreated the mentioned negative image of "the blood-stained Balkans" as something separated and alienated from the notion of civilised 'European'. This image was associated with the term 'Balkanisation': denoting division, violence, chaos, authoritarian regimes—against which a positive image of Europe and the West was constructed (Juncos 2005). In the words of Susan Sontag (2003, 71–72):

> That there could be death camps and a siege and civilians slaughtered by the thousands and thrown into mass graves on European soil fifty years after the end of the Second World War gave the war in Bosnia and the Serb campaign of killing in Kosovo their special, anachronistic interest. But one of the main ways of understanding the war crimes committed in Southeastern Europe in the 1990s has been to say that the Balkans, after all, were never really part of Europe.

The media helped create an image of the Balkan wars that are today seen as bloody, violent and primitive (Juncos 2005; Zupančič and Arbeiter 2016).[6] At this point, it must be noted that public opinion in EU member states was largely shaped by Anglo-Saxon media. Lindstorm (2003) and Juncos (2005) argue that political elites from the region itself also used—and are still using—the 'Balkanisation' theme as a political weapon to dismiss their competition or political enemies: detaching

---

[5]For more on the decentralisation and separation of Kosovar societal institutions, see Chap. 3: Kosovo in socialist Yugoslavia.

[6]Zupančič and Arbeiter (2016, 1060) write that, in comparison, the First Gulf War (1991) which started around the same time as the beginning of the dissolution of Yugoslavia and lasted for 17 days, has been portrayed as a "short and flawless operation". However, the number of victims in the First Gulf War, which is at least half the total number of war victims killed in the wars in former Yugoslavia, was created in 17 days only. The pace of brutality is thus hardly comparable. Moreover, the media forgot about the fact the Vietnam War resulted in 3 million deaths of Vietnamese people. Nevertheless, the journalist did not stop short of depicting the wars in the 1990s in former Yugoslavia as a consequence of the "ancient hate" and "brutality of the Balkans people".

themselves from the term by claiming to hold European aspirations, while presenting their neighbours or political competitors as representatives of 'the Balkans'
or being "balkanised". Zupančič and Arbeiter (2016) write that, especially during
the war, negative stereotyping was employed to promote the conflict: portraying
another nation as crude, violent and as blameworthy for their nation's misery.[7]

This negative image influenced how some countries presented themselves, such
as Slovenia, Croatia, Bulgaria and Romania, that sought to distance and detach
themselves from the region after gaining independence. However, neither the ideal
picture of multicultural cohabitation nor the negative stereotyping of the primitive
Balkans reflects the truth—a complex picture based on both ethnic tensions and
peaceful co-existence in the region (Juncos 2005).

Integration of this region into European structures might end this debate and
finally designate the region as European. Yet, due to the negative image of the
people in the region being primitive, by analogy, their economies should also be
backward, underdeveloped—this all strengthened the perception this area has no
place in a stable, peaceful and Europeanised continent—making the terms "the
Balkans" and "European integration" incompatible (Uvalic 1997, 19–34 in Juncos,
2005). Nevertheless, already after the wars in the 1990s the EU maintained the view
that all of the former Yugoslav countries had European prospects. This was a
consequence of the "hour of Europe" in the 1990s, discussed in the following
chapter, and the EU's efforts to be seen as a viable security and normative actor not
only in this region, but beyond.

3.1.1   "The Hour of Europe in the 1990s": The EU and the Breaking up of Yugoslavia

In the 1970s, Duchêne (1973, 43) talked about the EC's role in the world,
describing it as a "civilian power". This implies its influence goes beyond the use of
military force, but also applies diplomatic and economic instruments which he
believed are more important. Juncos (2005, 94) notes that "to be a civilian power,
the EU needed to eschew the use of force in international relations (implying
military instruments) and to pursue 'civilian' ends such as the promotion of
democracy, human rights, rule of law, and multilateralism". This was the role the
EC (later the EU) followed prior to the wars in former Yugoslavia and was also
pursued in wartime (1991–1995).

The outcomes of the events mentioned in the previous chapter—less strong
socialist regimes, economic and political crisis—weakened the idea that the SFRY

---

[7]As Zupančič and Arbeiter (2016) note, the problem of a stereotype is that it is self-fulfilling—
whoever perceives a certain stereotype as true will quickly notice certain behaviour that corresponds to this regional stereotype, but not the opposite behaviour (one who upsets the true image
or opposes it).

could persist in its multi-ethnic formation led by a central government (rotating presidency) while nationalism in the republics was gaining ground. Fuelled by the irredentist tensions and nationalist rhetoric, the Yugoslav identity and the political stability of the country were then further eroded by its political leaders. The first republics of the six to formally leave the SFRY were Slovenia and Croatia, both declaring their independence on 25 June 1991. While Slovenia's path to independence was comparatively short with a small number of causalities, Croatia's struggle for independence was more difficult. However, it was in Bosnia and Herzegovina—the most ethnically diverse country of all the Yugoslav republics, over which both Croatian and Serbian nationalisms maintained claims—where the armed conflict of the 1990s proved to be deadliest (Mahmutćehajić 2001, 139–145).

For the EC, the chaos in former Yugoslavia could not be ignored since it was practically taking place on its borders (Brenner 1992, 587). With the start of armed hostilities in 1991, the EC tried to find a negotiated solution. From today's perspective, it could be argued that this was one of the first difficult tests for the (then non-existing) CFSP. At the beginning of the crisis, the EC sent a high-level mediation team to Belgrade, aimed at bringing the Yugoslav Government and the 'rebel' republics of Slovenia and Croatia back to the negotiating table. Before leaving for the meeting in Belgrade, the Chair of Presidency of the Council of the EU Jacques Poos referred to the member states' high expectations regarding the development of the common foreign policy stance and the Community's responsibility to act in a crisis threatening European stability. "This is the hour of Europe", he said, "It is not the hour of the Americans" (ibid.). Calling attention to the European initiative that was independent of the USA, Poos expressed the feelings of expectation and hope that accompanied this self-conscious presentation of the Community's diplomatic self-reliance (Brenner 1992, 588). The EC therefore held a high profile at the start of the conflict, and put various diplomatic and economic sanctions in place. However, the issue of the recognition of the breakaway republics hampered those efforts as it did later on in the negotiations regarding the war in Croatia and Bosnia and Herzegovina (Juncos 2005).

After the meeting, the mediation team announced the parties had agreed to accept certain measures to end the conflict.[8] The Community warned it would suspend economic aid of almost USD 1 billion if the Yugoslav Government did not halt the Yugoslav People's Army's military operations against Slovenia and Croatia.[9] The breakaway republics, on the other hand, had to commit themselves to cease all activities related to independence. Last but not least, it has to be said that the EC wished to preserve Yugoslavia as a single political entity. This stance was also clearly repeated by the US administration on all possible occasions (Zupančič 2016).

---

[8]The then Prime Minister of SFRY Ante Marković, Slovenian President Milan Kučan and Croatian President Franjo Tuđman.

[9]Some authors (Woodward 1995) claim that some of the more effective instruments of the EC, such as economic assistance, were not used as a trump card before the crisis, but this case shows the Community actually used this 'ace'.

The European negotiation team offered assistance in redrafting the Yugoslav constitution to help retain a single entity and grant greater autonomy to both republics. Yet, the Community was not unanimous on the action due to disagreements over the importance it should have paid to the potentially contradictory principles of self-determination and territorial integrity. Germany argued for the right to self-determination of Slovenia and Croatia (probably due to the Christian Democratic Party of Germany's close ties with the Slovenian and Croatian Catholic parties). France stated that Yugoslavia's territorial integrity was a priority and this was supported by Great Britain, Italy and Spain (New York Times 1991; Zupančič 2016).

The Community's negotiators' first effort to end the armed hostilities was the Common Declaration on the Peaceful Resolution of the Yugoslav Crisis, also known as the Brioni Agreement. It was signed by the Slovenian authorities, the Yugoslav Government and the EC in July 1991. The EU-brokered agreement brought about a cease-fire which effectively stopped the war in Slovenia. However, it was then clear that the remains of former Yugoslavia, then dominated by Slobodan Milošević, were not so concerned with Slovenia leaving the federation (the ethnically relatively homogenous Slovenia had never appeared on maps of Great Serbia which, together with the maps of Great Croatia, paved the way to bloodshed). Although the EC's ministerial threesome, invoking the earliest elements of the common foreign policy, believed in the success of the Community's intervention it was soon clear a three-month moratorium on Slovenia's declaration of independence, as envisaged in the Brioni agreement, was not enough to prevent bloodshed; the Yugoslav People's Army and Serbian paramilitaries started to regroup in Croatia and Bosnia and Herzegovina, in preparation for continuation of the armed conflict (Helsinki Committee for Human Rights in Serbia 2016).

The EC sponsored the Hague Peace Conference in September 1991, namely the last attempt to preserve the Yugoslav single entity as a confederation or loose federation. Important for understanding the future war in Kosovo in 1998–1999 is the arbitration process known as the Badinter Commission.[10] It started work in November 1991. Its mandate was to resolve constitutional issues in dispute, such as who is eligible to declare independence under the Yugoslav Constitution of 1974 and who is not. The EC presented its view that the Yugoslav republics—and not *peoples* or so-called *autonomous regions* like Kosovo or Vojvodina—were those who could seek secession. The EC imposed a deadline by which republics could apply for recognition of their independence.

---

[10]The Arbitration Commission of the Conference on Yugoslavia (known as the Badinter Arbitration Commission) was set up by the Council of Ministers of the European Economic Community in 1991 to provide the Peace Conference on Yugoslavia with legal advice. The president of the five-member Commission, consisting of presidents of the Constitutional Courts in the EEC, was a French lawyer and professor called Robert Badinter. The Arbitration Commission produced opinions on major legal questions raised by the conflict between the republics of former SFRY (Radan 2000).

This was a turning point in European foreign policy and diplomacy. But, as a consequence of the Badinter Commission's findings, the EC did not support the claims of Kosovars for independence. Further, Macedonian independence was also not recognised due to Greece's objections following the unresolved dispute over the official name of the former Yugoslav country. The EC's recognition of Slovenia and Croatia was also delayed; it only came under the pressure of Germany in January 1992 after the brutal occupation and destruction of Vukovar and shelling of Dubrovnik by the Yugoslav People's Army and paramilitary troops, linked to the regime in Belgrade (ibid.).

This inability to act or agree on common action during the initial stages of violence in the region showed the limits of the coordination through then EPC mechanisms, as skilfully exploited by local protagonists in former Yugoslavia (Juncos 2005). The EC had several opportunities and means available, at least strong political pressure. Yet disagreements among the European actors themselves (the EC and EC member states) prevented any joint military action.

When the violence intensified, the EC was marginalised by the intervention of other actors, but continued to play a diplomatic and humanitarian role within the UN framework. In August 1992, the EC launched an International Conference on the former Yugoslavia in Geneva under the UN's auspices, and also supported and committed itself to implement a new regime of sanctions approved by the UNSC. This later proved to be detrimental for every party to the conflict in terms of self-defensive measures, except for the Yugoslav People's Army that was already heavily armed. The EC was also an important actor for humanitarian assistance and for supplying the United Nations Protection Force (UNPROFOR) mission in Bosnia and Herzegovina with troops (ibid.).

In 1994, five states established the Contact Group (the USA, the Russian Federation, France, Great Britain and Germany). Consisting of representatives of influential states, this group began leading international efforts to bring the conflict in the former SFRY to an end. This saw the EU's role significantly decrease. Today, Poos' reference to 'the Hour of Europe' even paradoxically symbolises what the EU failed to do in former Yugoslavia in terms of supranational action (Glaurdić 2011).

3.1.2   Seeking a Civilian Power Identity: The EU and Creation of "The Western Balkans"

In December 1995, the Dayton Peace Agreement was signed in Ohio in the USA, with the EU as an institution not playing any significant role. Namely, it was the influential states whose resolution to halt the hostilities culminated in NATO's military operation against the Yugoslav People's Army that brought the war to an end. However, the EU later gained new momentum and was given a major role by being put in charge of assisting the post-conflict reconstruction of war-torn territories. At the Madrid European Council in December 1995, the EU expressed its intention to implement the civilian aspects of the peace agreement using its strengths and capacities as a civilian power (Juncos 2005).

Learning from its failures during the initial period of war in former Yugoslavia and reacting to criticism of its inability to react in time, the EU launched the most extensive external involvement in the region in the form of post-conflict reconstruction and peacebuilding after the conflict. The region was also given the so-called European perspective to encourage the creation of states that would provide for stability in the region. The term "Western Balkans" was coined in the context of the Stabilisation and Association Process (SAP). The SAP was developed as a common framework governing relations with the Western Balkans up till their accession to the EU. This was the first instance in which the region was offered prospects of EU integration (WOSCAP 2017, 13).[11] The process has since become the dominant political goal of countries in the region following the dissolution of the socialist regimes in the SFRY and Albania. The term Western Balkans denotes the Balkan countries without Bulgaria and Romania, which "were left outside this security-political framework" (Dolenc et al. 2014, 66). After Croatia also joined the EU, the term stood for countries in South East Europe in principle eligible for EU membership: Bosnia and Herzegovina, Serbia, Montenegro, Macedonia, Albania, and Kosovo. Put shortly, the term is a genuine political label used specifically in the European integration process (ibid.).[12]

Aware of the Union's non-existing military capacities, EU officials believed that peacebuilding and other efforts of a non-coercive nature could become a credible means for the EU's external engagement and also 'a hallmark' of the institution. In Bosnia and Herzegovina, the EU adopted a civilian approach based on diplomatic and economic instruments. Apart from humanitarian assistance, Bosnia and Herzegovina benefited from trade preferences as well as the PHARE and OBNOVA

---

[11]The European Commission actually laid down the principles for the SAP in the context of the EU's inability to stop the violence during the war in Kosovo (WOSCAP 2017, 13). This happened in the Communication to the Council and the European Parliament in May 1999, which was confirmed by the Council in June 1999. The content of the SAP contained the development of Stabilisation and Association Agreements, a form of contractual relationship, including the individual situation of each Western Balkans country. The Agreement offers the prospect of EU membership once the Copenhagen criteria are met. Next, it offered the development of economic relations within the region, the reorientation and development of the existing economic assistance, increased assistance for governance, democratisation, education, institution-building, civil society. Moreover, the SAP brought a promise of new opportunities for cooperation in other fields, such as justice and home affairs, as well as the development of political dialogue, including dialogue at the regional level (ibid.).

[12]It otherwise connects countries of diverse political, historical and social backgrounds, which are coincidentally geographically close and were part of socialist regimes, but have entered the new millennium even more diverse and divided than after the World War II. The Western Balkans is nowadays also the poorest region of Europe, with 30–40% of the EU-28 GDP average, but its countries differ in their socio-economic and political context (ibid.). Dolenc and others (2014, 68) argue that while the process of European integration is the source of the convergence process, these differences lead us to expect substantial divergence in performance with respect to the reforms they should conduct in the process.

programmes, which established the basis for political and economic conditionality (respect for human rights, democracy, and rule of law). Therefore, in 1997 the EU started emphasising the normative aspects of its involvement in the Western Balkans in its regional approach to encouraging cooperation and the region's long-term structural perspective (Juncos 2005).

Conversely, NATO's military intervention that effectively ended the war in Bosnia and Herzegovina and the successive NATO military presence in the country was more of a short-term and 'tougher' approach. This allowed the EU a secondary role in the region, while re-enforcing the status of NATO as the leading provider of security in Europe. The EU was limited to providing economic assistance under the auspices of the UN (ibid.). However, after the events in Kosovo, and the St. Malo Summit in 1998, this EU approach would start to change when the UK and France agreed on the need to develop the EU's military capabilities (Wouters and Naert 2004, 35).

Since the St. Malo Declaration, the use of military force has been included in the EU's toolbox of conflict prevention capabilities and considered necessary for effective external action. Pilegaard (2004, 19) notes that "the EU's contribution as a civilian power arguably presupposes the existence of a military power, able and willing to pave the way for subsequent civilian efforts to have an impact". The EU back then had to depend on the USA for this military support, but made an effort to address its lack of military power by developing a stronger European capacity to project military force (ibid.).

Manners' (in Juncos 2005, 98) analysis of the EU's involvement in Bosnia and Herzegovina shows the EU's preference to use civilian instruments and long-term structural approaches to conflict prevention. The EU claimed it is concerned with the root causes of the conflict, instead of simply bringing a certain conflict to an end. The latter peace-enforcement approach is essentially conditioned by having strong military capabilities at its disposal, instead of 'only' keeping the peace. Yet once it started to develop its military component, the EU could no longer argue that the institution could be seen only as a normative power in the Balkans.

The main lesson arising from the conflict in Bosnia and Herzegovina was that "if the EU wanted to be a credible and effective international actor and a promoter of norms in its neighbouring area, it needed to be able to back up its diplomacy with military coercion" (Juncos 2005, 99). And, indeed, at the beginning of the new century, the EU finally resorted also to military means—Bosnia and Herzegovina was selected as the "real test of the first ESDP missions, the first ever EU Police Mission in January 2003 and the largest EU military mission, EUFOR Althea, to date" (Juncos 2005, 88).

3.2   Kosovo: A Problem in the EU's Immediate Vicinity

Since the beginning of the wars in Slovenia and later in Croatia and Bosnia and Herzegovina, the focus of the EC and the member states was on maintaining peace and stability in the region. The war in Kosovo (1998–1999) was the final phase of violence surrounding the disintegration of former Yugoslavia. However, it was also in Kosovo where the first signs of Yugoslav political instability were clearly visible: one should remember the demonstrations of Kosovo Albanian students demanding more rights and better conditions in 1981. Nevertheless, fully-fledged war in Kosovo did not erupt in the early 1990s, as was the case in Slovenia, Croatia, and Bosnia and Herzegovina. But while political entities with the legal status of republics achieved statehood early in the 1990s, Kosovo, on the other hand, remained under the jurisdiction of Belgrade despite the clear desires of Kosovo Albanians who wanted their own state (Zupančič 2015).

Led by President Slobodan Milošević, the authorities in Serbia fiercely ruled this option out. They claimed that Kosovo had never held the status of a republic—which would theoretically provide the right to secession according to the Badinter Commission—and that Kosovo is a cradle of Serbian statehood, the heart of Serbia, and its national soul (ibid.). Tensions between the Albanians and the Serbs in Kosovo escalated throughout the 1990s, until full-scale war broke out in 1998. The war continued until the ceasefire, followed by the withdrawal of the Yugoslav Armed Forces and Serbian-Montenegrin paramilitary troops in June 1999, which was a direct consequence of the NATO military operation against FRY from March until June 1999 (Judah 2002).

The end of the war in Kosovo presented a new opportunity for the EU to introduce itself as a strong peacebuilding actor able to use its normative power to influence the country's reconstruction and become credited as 'a force for good'. The central point of the EU's engagement in the Western Balkans has since then been aimed at Kosovo because back then the other countries of the region seemed to be on the path to stabilisation.

The current conflict in Kosovo has significantly different dimensions to the nature of the armed conflict in the territory during the 1990s. This is precisely why one needs to understand the background to the complicated relationship between the Albanians and Serbs in Kosovo. Without observing and knowing about the root causes of the conflict, the role of EULEX and its role in support of building and reforming the judiciary, a multi-ethnic police and customs service in Kosovo, which makes up the core of this book, cannot be understood properly. This is the main reason why the next subchapters analyse the root causes of the conflict in Kosovo.

3.2.1 The Period Before the War in Kosovo

Navigating between Historical Facts and Myth

The Albanian-Serbian conflict is a conflict marked by the infamous question of *who was in this territory first* and who, as a result, holds the *historical right* to not only inhabit but exclusively manage the territory. The dilemma of 'who is first' and the historical arguments—from which the myths derive from—have been used countless times in political battles between the two peoples. While the argument of Serbs builds on their right to inhabit the territory of the Serbian medieval kingdom—the symbol of unification of their ancestors, descendants and God, as they believe—the argument of the Kosovo Albanians finds its basis in ethnogenesis, claiming to be of Illyrian origin and therefore 'there first'—or, at least, before the Slavs (ibid.).

Historically speaking, the tribe of Illyrians which in the 4th century BC inhabited the territory of what is today Kosovo, spoke a language similar to Albanian. On the other hand, the Serbs, a nation of South Slavic origin, settled in the Balkan Peninsula in the 5th and 6th centuries when the last remnants of the Roman Empire's authority were disappearing from the area (King and Mason 2006, 26). At the time, the Balkan Peninsula was a conglomerate of different tribal groups moving around the area in their search of territory and related resources.

The transition from the 1st to 2nd millennium brought new challenges for the territory of today's Kosovo. The Byzantine Empire ruled here between 1014 and 1018, but did not last long. Two centuries later, at the start of the 13th century, a new force formed north of Kosovo—the Serbian dynasty of Nemanjić—which conquered the territory and triggered a cultural and religious boom in Kosovo. The area saw the construction of the first monasteries and, at the end of the 13th century, the seat of the Orthodox Church was transferred to Peja/Peć (today the most important city in the western part of Kosovo).

Between 1331 and 1346, the medieval Serbian state was ruled by king Stefan Dušan, also known as Dušan the Mighty. His kingdom centred in Skopje expanded to some parts of what is today' Montenegro (Bar), Macedonia (Epirus), Albania (Valoro), Greece (Thessaly) and Kosovo (Prizren). Albanian nobility helped King Dušan win over Epirus and Thessaly; the nobility was also an active factor in the Serbian state. The king of state, which spread from the Danube to Corinth in modern Greece, was even called "the ruler of the Serbs and the Greeks" by the patriarch of the Serbian Orthodox Church (Drançolli 1984, 29–31; Krstić 2006, 28).

However, the Serbian rulers were soon forced to acknowledge the superiority of a certain emerging power in the neighbourhood. It was the Ottomans who began consolidating their rule in the Balkans in the 14th century following the Serbian army's defeat in the battle of Maritsa in 1371 and continuing with invasion of the Serbian kingdom (Malcolm 1999; Krstić 2006). Within a few decades, the Ottoman Empire had conquered the entire Balkan Peninsula. Historical sources bring us testimonies of Albanian rebellions against the conquering army in which Serbian nobles also participated (Drançolli 1984, 31). The combined armed forces of the Serbs and Albanians managed to defeat them in the area of the present-day Montenegro. After the defeat, Sultan Murad I started to build up a massive army to take revenge, ultimately leading to the battle at Kosovo Polje in 1389 (Weller 2009, 25).

The Battle at Kosovo Polje and the "500 Years of Injustice" Argument
The battle at Kosovo Polje supposedly took place on 28 June 1389, not far from modern-day Prishtina (Malcolm 1999). Historical sources are quite short in credible information about the battle, but concur that the Serbian local commander, Prince Stefan Lazar Hrebeljanović, did not want to surrender to the Ottoman Empire. Instead of giving in, he took up arms against the Ottoman army. A week prior to the battle, he established an interesting coalition to fight the Ottomans. Namely, he

invited the Albanians into the coalition, together with the Serbs, Bosnians and certain other so-called Christian armies. The fact they all fought shoulder to shoulder against the Ottomans is not something many people in Serbia or Kosovo are glad to be reminded of (Weller 2009, 25; Drançolli 2008, 38–39).

The Ottomans were the winners of this battle that reshaped the history of this part of South East Europe (Voje 1994, 114). Despite the Ottoman victory, the Serbs retained some sort of control over Kosovo for the next few decades, during which time most of the feudal lords became Ottoman vassals. Yet the situation changed in 1459 when the Ottomans obtained complete control over the area (Ruvarac 1992). The battle itself was not particularly important in military terms, and was not particularly well-known throughout history until the 1980s when details of the battle were 'rediscovered' for political purposes (yet it should be noted that Kosovo 'existed' in Serb literature as an important place of remembrance). Referring to this very battle, Slobodan Milošević, aided by a considerable share of the Serbian cultural and intellectual elites, managed to build a myth around it that presented the Kosovo battle in terms of "the Serbs against the rest" or as a struggle of justice against evil (Malcolm 1999).

Like Prince Lazar's decision to fight the Ottoman sultan was based on an alleged struggle to choose between the 'earthly kingdom of power and comfort, but without pride' on one hand and the 'heavenly realm of eternal justice' on the other, the Serbian elites also saw modern Serbia's struggle for the conquest of Kosovo as the same. Long before Milošević rose to power, Popović (1976) pointed out that some historical facts about the battle of Kosovo had been completely intertwined with fake and mythological content. This kind of merging history and fiction represents a new danger for those unable or unwilling to recognise what is true and what is made up in this story.

During the Ottoman occupation of the Balkans, most Albanians—until then predominantly Christian—slowly embraced Islam as their religion. This was also due to existential calculations since Muslims were not obliged to pay taxes to the Ottomans. This put them in a privileged position (Drançolli 1984, 40–47; Ruvarac 1992; King and Mason 2006, 26). Nevertheless, some Albanians remained loyal to their original faith (predominantly Orthodox and Catholic). This internal divorce within a single nation that led to the emergence of two or even three faiths is thought to have contributed to the Albanian national consciousness' relatively late development. Another element was the inconsistent use of alphabets: in the south of the ethnic Albanian territory the Greek alphabet was used, while Latin was used in the north. Moreover, some Albanians used Arabic writing as a sign of respect for Islam (King and Mason 2006, 26–29).

Albanian communities were known for their quite isolated life in certain remote areas that had practically not been reached by the Turkish authorities. Thus, some traditional laws were preserved, the best known certainly being the Kanun of Lekë Dukagjini (*Kanun Lek*). This practice of oral laws was preserved in some places until the mid-20th century. The law encompassed practically all areas of social life, including blood revenge (*hakmarrje*). Blood revenge in practice meant a man could kill a person who had seriously offended or humiliated him. Moreover, even a close male relative of the person humiliated could carry out the vengeance, which might also be imposed on a family member of the one committing the original 'crime'.

Horrible circles of revenge have often dragged on for decades, causing some families to build proper fortresses to prevent revenge, while possible targets of retaliation have been forcibly detained in them (King and Mason 2006, 28). Some people have practically disappeared from public eye due to this practice. Unsurprisingly, in the late 1980s and early 1990s intellectual elites in Serbia often argued that this practice, which is nowadays limited, shows the Albanians lag behind in civilisational terms (Zupančič 2015).

While the Albanians gradually adapted to Ottoman rule, the Serbs did not feel at ease in the late 17th century and *en masse* started to leave the area of Kosovo for central Serbia. One of the motivating factors to move north included the desire to help the Austrian army liberate Serbia from Ottoman domination. Unfortunately for the Serbs, the Habsburg army was defeated. After troops of the Habsburg Empire withdrew, the Serbs became the target of the Ottomans' cruel revenge (Weller 2009, 26).

Some authors (Jelavich 1983; Vickers 1997) understand these migrations of the Serbs as the beginnings of a change in the ethnic composition of Kosovo—in favour of the Albanians and at the expense of the Serbs. All this led to the awakening of Serbian national identity in the early 19th century. As a direct consequence, a series of Serbian uprisings (*ustanak*) against the Ottomans followed (Zupančič 2015, 52). In 1844, Ilija Garašanin, a well-known politician and statesman, who was also the Minister of the Interior and the Prime Minister of the Serbian Government, published the political manifesto *Načertanije*. The document for the first time contained clear Serbian claims for some territories in the Balkans. Certain observers claim *Načertanije* represents the start of the Great Serbia idea, later harnessed by aggressive Serbian politicians in the 1990s (ibid.).

From the Congress of Berlin to the end of the World War II (1878–1945)
An important turning point for Kosovar territory came in 1878, when the Congress of Berlin was held. The European Great Powers then recognised the right of statehood to Serbia and Montenegro. Pan-Slavic and Orthodox sympathies for the Slavic nations from imperial Russia played an important role here. On the other hand, the Albanian requests for statehood were largely ignored. Just four years later (1882), Serbia proclaimed its independence and also demanded the accession of Kosovo to its territory, then still under Ottoman rule (Weller 2009, 26). By completely ignoring the Albanians' demands for statehood, the Berlin Congress is one of their darkest moments in recent history (Rrecaj 2006).

With the Ottoman Empire's dissolution and the rise of Serbia, the desire of the Albanians to have their own state was growing. To help facilitate this aspiration, the Albanians founded the League of Prizren, a political assembly that sought to unite all Albanian-populated areas within a single autonomous unit (Glenny 2001). The Prizren League demanded that all state officials speak Albanian, and that local authorities be put in charge of managing at least one part of the taxes collected.

The Albanian aspirations grew bigger when the Turkish Empire disintegrated and, during the anti-Turkish riots in 1912, turned into a request for complete independence. The Balkan wars followed in which Serb-Montenegrin units, helped by Bulgaria and Greece, defeated the remaining Turkish troops and conquered Kosovo and central Macedonia.[13] The Treaty of Bucharest (1913) legalised this new reality on the ground and so the territory of Serbia expanded from 18,650 to 33,891 square kilometres—and Kosovo *de iure* became part of Serbia (Skendi 1953).

When World War I erupted in 1914 and the Central Powers attacked Serbia, the Battle at Kosovo Polje of 1389 started to become glorified in Belgrade. When the Serbian army had to retreat from their positions and find shelter elsewhere, a few hundred thousand Serbian civilians fled with them. The only escape was to the south: this meant crossing the territory of central Serbia, through Kosovo and Montenegro to Albania and the island of Corfu. King Peter with his family, along with the army and scores of civilians, also fled along this path. In addition to a harsh winter, attacks by groups of Albanians obstructed their retreat. The attacks and extreme weather conditions saw some 200,000 to 240,000 Serbs lose their lives. This level of "hospitality" only deepened the grievances between the two nations (Ćorović 1993, 583–585).

The Paris Peace Conference (1919–1920) reaffirmed that Kosovo was a constitutive part of the Kingdom of Serbs, Croats and Slovenians despite opposition to this 'solution' from the Albanians from Kosovo. Serbia succeeded to convince the winners of World War I, who were legitimising the new world order at the Paris Conference, to recognise its right to Kosovo, which since the Balkan wars in 1912–1913 had been under Serbian control. Great Britain and France in particular were sympathetic to the Serbian arguments that Serbia needed Kosovo to recover from the trauma it had suffered during World War I (King and Mason 2006, 32).

However, Albanian national consciousness was already well formed. In 1921, the Kosovo Albanians handed a petition to the League of Nations to let Kosovo join Albania (King and Mason 2006, 32). They referred to the argument the Albanian identity was under threat in the new political formation because, according to their estimates, the Serbs had killed 12,371 inhabitants of Kosovo from 1918 to 1921 and imprisoned another 22,000 (Vickers 1997). The League of Nations did not approve the Albanians' request.

Zejnullah Gruda (in Rrecaj 2006, 14) thus claims that at that time Kosovo became a synonym for the denial of fundamental human rights. The concealment of resistance, which occasionally turned into aggression against the Albanians,

---

[13]Reports of the time talk of the crimes against the Albanian population in this period (Weller 2009; Krstić 2006). Lampe (1996, 97) states the Serbian army justified the crimes referring to the expulsion of 150,000 Serbs from Kosovo from 1870 onwards. A reporter from the Pravda newspaper and later Bolshevik revolutionary Lev Trotsky mentioned the words of the Serbian officer in his report "Soon after crossing the border with Kosovo, we witnessed atrocities: the whole Albanian villages turned into fiery pillars; property and settlements where their fathers and grandfathers lived disappeared in flames. These scenes were reproduced on our way to Skopje, where the Serbs went to the Turkish and Albanian houses and prey and kill…" (Trotsky in King and Mason 2006, 31). The international public was not well acquainted with the crimes of the Serbian army and paramilitary in the Balkan wars.

manifested in various forms. It is worth mentioning the plan of the Serbian intellectual Vasa Čubrilović in 1937 that proposed to expel Albanians from Kosovo and settle the territory with Serbs (Rrecaj 2006, 19; Elsie 2017).

During World War II, the majority of Kosovo Albanians saw an opportunity to do away with the 'Slavic state' forever and join up with 'the mother-state Albania'. Albania had already been invaded by the fascist Italian troops in 1939 and functioned as an Italian protectorate governed by the fascist puppet governments of Shefqet Vërlaci (1939–1941) and Mustafa-Merlika Kruja (1941–1943). Unsurprisingly, the Albanians of Kosovo retaliated against the Serbs in large numbers (Pearson 2006, 167).

But at the end of World War II it was the Serbs who emerged victorious. It was almost impossible to believe they could forgive what they called the Albanians' opportunistic approach during the war. Consequently, the Serbs' revenge was fierce when they gained momentum at the end of war, after the defeated forces withdrew. The area was soon occupied by Tito's partisans that soon began retaliating against the Albanian 'collaborators'. The Partisans especially attacked the Albanian organisation Balli Kombëtar which, after the capitulation of Italy in 1943, entered the service of the Third Reich. Serious violence triggered a rebellion of the Albanians, which lasted for a couple of months. In response, no fewer than 30,000 partisans were sent to Kosovo to violently suppress the resistance (Nečak 1984, 193–200; Weller 2009, 28).

Kosovo in Socialist Yugoslavia
An important year for understanding the conflict in Kosovo is 1945 when World War II finally ended. It was then that the Serbian National Assembly proclaimed Kosovo as an autonomous region within Serbia. The common interest of the Communist Party of the SFRY and the Albanian Communist Party—the two parties fighting fascism and Nazism in their respective countries—contributed to the idea of the two countries merging to become more effective and respected in the international arena. In addition, some other interesting ideas were floated before and after World War II, for example, the confederative idea of merging Yugoslavia, Albania, Bulgaria, Turkey and Greece to create a 'Balkan Federation' based on a leftist ideology. This idea never took off as the USSR did not support the move (Stanič 1984, 56; Dranqoli 2011).

In 1946, at a Special Plenary session of the Central Committee of the Communist Party of Albania party leader Enver Hoxha asked whether the SFRY should be required to allow the accession of Kosovo to Albania and then proceed with merging Yugoslavia and Albania. He himself then replied that such an idea is not advanced, because "democratic Yugoslavia is more advanced than we are /.../ and it is in our own interest that Yugoslavia is strong, since having a strong democratic SFRY will mean that democracy will prevail also in other parts of the Balkans". Ideas about merging remained in circulation for some time, but fell apart after Tito's dispute with Stalin in 1948 (the Informbiro crisis). The Albanian leadership had to choose between Tito and Stalin; it chose the Soviet option and accused Yugoslavia of 'betraying socialism' while cancelling all agreements with the country in the same year. These political changes also sealed Kosovo's fate within the SFRY (Stanič 1984, 56; Dranqoli 2011).

According to the new legislation, Kosovo became one of two autonomous provinces of Serbia within Yugoslavia. The post-war period was, among others, characterised by repression and the migration of tens of thousands of Albanians mostly to Turkey (Mertus 1999; Weller 2009). They were especially encouraged to do so by the third strongest political figure in the SFRY Aleksandar Ranković and his group;[14] the Albanians were offered a simplified procedure for changing nationality and issuing documents when departing for Turkey. The number of Yugoslav citizens who emigrated to Turkey rose: from 1953 to 1966 more than 230,000 people left for Turkey; more of 80% were of Albanian descent (Radio Free Europe 1983; Hoxha 1984, 214).

In the 1960s, the situation of Kosovo Albanians improved somewhat and they demanded more political rights. A glimpse of a freer society was also enabled as a result of Tito's purge of Ranković and his allies in 1966. In 1968, the Albanians of Kosovo organised mass protests, shocking the political leadership of the SFRY; the slogan "Kosovo Republic" was first heard at these demonstrations and made for a sobering moment for the leadership regarding the (un)success of the politics of 'fraternity and unity'. Gradually, the political rights of Kosovo Albanians have been expanding. In 1969, a new statute for Kosovo was issued, further expanding the autonomy of the province (Radio Free Europe 1983; Meier 2005, 27; Boer and van der Borgh 2011).

Another milestone for the Albanians of Kosovo was the establishment of the University of Prishtina in 1970, when the Albanians were given a chance to study in their mother tongue at university level for the first time in history (Radio Free Europe 1983; Boer and van der Borgh 2011, 72). The Kosovo Albanians gained more rights in 1974. This year is perceived as one of the most important milestones in the modern history of Kosovo (and Yugoslavia) since it was when the new Yugoslav Constitution entered into force. Pursuant to it, Kosovo acquired almost the same rights as the six 'constitutive republics of Yugoslavia': Slovenia, Croatia, Bosnia and Herzegovina, Serbia, Montenegro and Macedonia (Meier 2005).

In this period, Kosovo acquired its own constitution, provincial parliament and provincial government. Although this was a step further for the rights of Albanians in Yugoslavia, Kosovo—as an autonomous province—did not gain the right to succeed from Yugoslavia. This important right remained 'reserved' for the republics only, contrary to the wishes of the Kosovo Albanians (Weller 2009). After 1974, the cultural identity of Kosovo Albanians started to grow as well. Educational and cultural institutions were established and the Albanians as a nation started to become more organised, creating dissatisfaction among the Serbs. The

---

[14]After World War II, Aleksandar Ranković served as Yugoslav minister of the interior and chief of the notorious intelligence agency UDBA (*Uprava državne bezbednosti*). He was stripped of power in 1966 upon accusations of bugging Tito's private premises (Radio Free Europe 1983).

demographics of Kosovo also started to change in favour of Albanians—at the expense of Serbs (Islami 1994).

In 1981, violent protests broke out at the University of Prishtina due to the harsh economic circumstances and unfair treatment of Albanians. These protests were quickly used by Kosovar politicians demanding more rights; this time, they requested that Kosovo's status be raised from autonomous region to a republic. The trigger of the demonstrations, which altered the political situation in Kosovo, was somewhat peculiar. Namely, an Albanian student allegedly found a cockroach in the soup in the university canteen; not surprisingly, the news quickly spread and protests began (Mertus 1999; Zupančič 2015).

The police intervened quickly and arrested some leaders of the protest. Now joined by ordinary citizens, the students demanded the release of those arrested. Protests by several thousand Kosovo Albanians were then given a new dimension: while initially demanding improved conditions at the university, they now called for better living conditions throughout the whole province of Kosovo. In two weeks, similar protests occurred in Prizren and again in Prishtina. The authorities declared an emergency, leading to the deployment of some 30,000 soldiers of the Yugoslav army and police forces to Kosovo. But the Kosovo Albanians continued to take to the streets, demanding a decent life and the proclamation of the Republic of Kosovo. Some went even further, calling for unification with Albania (Mertus 1999, 31).

The Yugoslav security apparatus responded fiercely in its attempt to suppress 'the nationalistic rebellion'. Support for the rights of Albanians in Kosovo also came from certain other republics opposed to the politics of the authorities in Belgrade. Slovenia in particular was allied with the "Kosovo cause" (Zupančič 2015). However, the repression of the Kosovo Albanians continued. In 1981, 60% of all political prisoners in Yugoslavia were ethnic Albanians. The authorities justified this repressive response by stating that Kosovo Albanians were responsible for the increasingly difficult situation of the Serbs in Kosovo (displacement of Serbs from state services, the poor economic situation etc.) (Mertus 1999, 97).

The Serbs' enormous dissatisfaction with the situation in Kosovo was enshrined in the Memorandum of the Serbian Academy of Science and Art from 1986. It stated the Serbs in Kosovo had been forced to endure "physical, political, legal and cultural genocide" (Srpska akademija nauka i umetnosti 1986). The grievances of many Serbs throughout the SFRY deepened. Hence, it is no surprise the disappointed Serbs became easy prey for the President of the Serbian Communist Party Slobodan Milošević, until then a well-known opponent of all forms of nationalism (King and Mason 2006, 36).

His political mentor Ivan Stambolić, President of the Republic of Serbia, sent Milošević to Kosovo on 24 April 1987 to address the demands of the ever more dissatisfied Kosovo Serbs. At that time, he uttered the (in)famous words: "No one is allowed to beat you [the Serbs]!" (King and Mason 2006, 36). Those words, together with the alleged understanding of the problems faced by Serbs in Kosovo, propelled Milošević into Serbian political orbit. This sentence heralded a new political discourse: while previously based on socialism, from now on nationalism was gaining ground (van der Borgh 2012, 35). The unhappy Kosovo Serbs became Milošević's 'shock troops' at around 100 events called 'Meetings of the Truth', massive pro-Serbian nationalistic protests against the alleged promotion of Kosovo's independence by the Albanians, which strengthened the Serbian image of the Serbs being the victims of historical injustice. The alleged trauma was later popularised as "The 500 years of injustice" argument (Zupančič 2015, 59).

To keep his promise to the Kosovo Serbs, Milošević abolished the autonomy of Kosovo in 1989. He managed to do so by initially forcing the governments of Vojvodina and Montenegro to resign in 1988, and then by putting in place puppet governments supportive of his brand of politics. He did the same in Kosovo when a new, favourable political leadership was put in power in Prishtina; the Serbian political leadership succeeded in removing the pro-Albanian leader of the Communist Party of Kosovo, Azem Vllasi, and assigned Rahman Morina to the position. Vllasi was also arrested in January 1989 on the basis he had been involved in preparing the demonstrations and strikes by Kosovo Albanians (Zupančič 2015, 60).

In response to Belgrade's political manoeuvring, Kosovo Albanians started a strike that shook the very foundations of socialist Yugoslavia and echoed across the country. Almost 2000 miners working in the Trepča/Stari trg mine near Kosovska Mitrovica started protesting against Milošević and his allies. Many miners closed themselves off within the mine, claiming they would not come to the surface until the SFRY started to respect the rights of the Kosovo Albanians (Zupančič 2013, 163–164).

Protests against Milošević and his circles continued in 1989 and the Serbs of Kosovo wanted more protection from the state authorities. It has to be acknowledged that several Serbs in Kosovo and their property were attacked by the Albanians on various occasions. Milošević promised the Kosovo Serbs full protection in a nationalistic speech delivered in Gazimestan at Kosovo Polje close to Prishtina. The speech on 28 June 1989, a day celebrated throughout Serbia as Saint Vitus Day (Vidovdan), was organised on the occasion of the 600th anniversary of the battle in Kosovo Polje (1389). After this event, extensive police actions followed and many Kosovo Albanians who had organised the protests against the regime in Belgrade ended up in prisons. Due to these political tensions, 23 Albanian activists (mostly intellectuals) founded the Democratic League of Kosovo. Dr Ibrahim Rugova, a pacifist professor and literary critic, who later became the president of Kosovo, was elected the party's president (Zupančič 2015, 60–61).

3.2.2   The SFRY's Dissolution, the War in Kosovo and NATO's Military Operation Against the FRY (1991–1999)

On 22 September 1991, the Albanians in Kosovo held a referendum on Kosovo's political future. Declared illegal by the authorities in Belgrade, the referendum saw 99% of Kosovo residents, mostly Albanians, vote for the independence of Kosovo.

'The will of the nation' was reaffirmed by members of the Kosovo Assembly in October 1991 who declared Kosovo an independent republic (Surroi 1997; King and Mason 2006, 39; Rogel 2003, 173).

Although the political structures in Serbia did not consider this political move of the Kosovo Albanians as either legal or legitimate, the Albanians started to establish parallel structures to address their basic needs: schools, health institutions, tax collection system etc. The main reason for the emergence of these parallel structures was the Albanians' claim they had been discriminated or even threatened in the existing state institutions, then mostly led by the Serbs; some claimed that Serbian doctors and nurses had 'treated' Kosovo Albanians in such a way their health deteriorated or they even died due to suspicious treatment methods (Bekaj 2010, 12; Kubo 2010, 1138).

Different ideas on how to achieve independence were discussed by the Kosovo Albanians. One part of the nation led by Ibrahim Rugova promoted a peaceful path, while the other thought that peaceful means—finding a political solution with Belgrade—had already been exhausted. This led to the establishment of the KLA that gained wider support only after the Dayton Agreement was adopted in 1995, when the 'Kosovo question' once again remained unsolved. The document that effectively ended the war in Bosnia and Herzegovina came as a great disappointment for the Kosovo Albanians since they believed their fate would also have been settled then. Rugova's peaceful policy, according to which the international community would put pressure on Serbia in favour of Kosovo, became less and less popular among the Kosovo Albanians as the oppression of them continued or even worsened (Mulaj 2008, 1106–1108; Kubo 2010).

Events Leading to War and Conflict
What tipped the scales in favour of finally transforming the KLA from a group of 'dissatisfied youth' to a paramilitary force was the crash of the 'financial pyramids' in Albania in 1997. The collapse of pyramid schemes, a fraudulent business model that promised its members huge profits, meant many Albanian citizens lost all their hard-earned savings (Bekaj 2010, 19). Consequently, Kosovo's neighbouring country of Albania descended into chaos: the borders became even more porous, military warehouses were broken into, the country became flooded with weapons and with many of them being smuggled over the mountains to Kosovo, where demand was high (Kubo 2010, 1143).

The first uniformed members of the KLA appeared in the Drenica region—a relatively remote and poor region in central Kosovo. They soon began to build their rising power and the trust of their oppressed compatriots at mass burials of KLA members killed in clashes with the armed forces of the FRY and paramilitary troops. In some cases, up to 20,000 people turned up at such funerals (Mulaj 2008; Kubo 2010).

The conflict escalated in 1998 when the Yugoslav armed forces killed Adem Jashari and 58 other Kosovo Albanians—many of them Jashari's relatives—in Prekaze, a small town near today's Skenderaj (Srbica) in the region of Drenica. The spirited resistance shown by Jashari, *komandanti legjendar* (»legendary commander «), is nowadays remembered and celebrated throughout Kosovo as one of the most heroic acts in the Kosovo Albanian's struggle against the Serbs. The open aggression not only had a significant impact on the Albanians from Kosovo, but also from Albania who became even more keen to join the KLA. Adopted on 23 September 1998, UNSC Resolution 1199 requested the immediate end of the armed conflict and an improvement in the humanitarian situation (Zupančič 2013, 163–169).

In October 1998, NATO threatened to bomb the FRY if its armed forces and paramilitary units did not pull out of Kosovo. To demonstrate his alleged preparedness to negotiate with the Kosovo Albanians and the international community, Milošević allowed observers from the OSCE to visit Kosovo. However, the violence in the province did not cease. The trigger event for NATO's intervention was a massacre in the Kosovar village of Reçak/Račak in early 1999 when almost 50 civilians were found executed. France, Germany, Great Britain, the USA, Italy and the Russian Federation proposed the Rambouillet Agreement, which the FRY refused to accept.

NATO then fulfilled its threat and on 24 March 1999 launched the military operation Allied Force against the FRY (King and Mason 2006, 44–5; Mulaj 2008, 1113). Throughout the military campaign against the FRY, NATO's leaders repeatedly emphasised the offensive's objectives, which Milošević was required to accept. The 11-week aerial offensive was not authorised by the UNSC. The Russian Federation and China, the two countries that had stood beside Milošević, made it clear they would have vetoed any proposal for military action against the FRY (Daskalovski 2003).

NATO's determination to carry out the military operation weakened several times during the process as the air strikes did not initially bring the desired effects. The Yugoslav army, after the NATO bombings started, began to blame Albanian civilians for the NATO strikes; hence, the KLA was no longer the main target of the regime, but civilians. The military operation against the FRY was less effective in a military sense than it could have been had the alliance's military aircraft operated at lower altitudes. This was, however, forbidden also due to a fear for the safety of the NATO personnel. NATO also made some drastic mistakes that partly discredited the alliance in the eyes of the international community (Simić 2000; Weller 2009, 166).

For example, supposedly by mistake, NATO attacked a convoy of refugees on tractors and trains in Kosovo, killing scores of civilians. In addition to the "collateral damage" alleged by NATO spokesman Jamie Shea, the bombing of the Chinese Embassy in Belgrade—again, supposedly a mistake—resonated strongly in the international community (Weller 2009, 166). Only a few believe NATO's official interpretation that the cause of the incorrect bombing of the Chinese Embassy was the old military maps NATO had used when choosing a target (Simić 2000; Weller 2009).

Sweeney et al. (1999) in a report based on interviews with senior NATO officials (whose identities are not disclosed) argue that NATO deliberately attacked the Chinese Embassy after NATO's electronic intelligence system detected certain signals (relevant information) were being sent to the FRY's military units from the embassy area. Three NATO officers acknowledged they knew the Chinese Embassy in Belgrade had provided a transmitter to the armed forces of the FRY after the FRY army's own transmitters were destroyed in April 1999 by NATO bombing. The Chinese also supposedly monitored incoming NATO missiles, helping the Yugoslav army combat them more effectively. Another speculation concerning the bombing is the belief that the Serbs had promised China—in return for helping to resist NATO—the remnants of the F-117 military aircraft and its advanced stealth technology that had been shot down by the Yugoslav army.

Throughout the armed conflict, diplomats were working to find a solution to end the hostilities. The hostilities between NATO and the FRY ceased after 78 days when a Military-Technical Agreement was signed by the two parties. Also known as the Kumanovo Agreement, the ceasefire was accepted on 9 June 1999 and called for the gradual withdrawal from Kosovo of the Yugoslav units and paramilitaries linked to them. It also envisaged the deployment of NATO troops in the province and the establishment of a so-called buffer zone. The demilitarised zone included 5 kilometres of Serbian territory (measured from the Kosovo border) and FRY troops were prohibited from entering it (Weller 2009, 176–179).

The FRY *de facto* lost control over Kosovo as all of its institutions, including the armed forces, had to leave the province. Despite many discussions following NATO's unauthorised use of force, the decision is today considered a turning point in understanding of human rights and international law. Namely, several scholars and members of the international community have started to believe that the mass violation of human rights, such as what happened in Kosovo, should no longer be viewed as an internal matter of a sovereign state but that it has an international dimension. The sacrosanct principle of a state's exclusive sovereignty over its territory—and the people living there—has come under question. While chiefly explained as "a humanitarian intervention", the air strikes quickly led to development of the concept Responsibility to Protect (Bellamy 2008).

The political and scholarly debate on whether the NATO military campaign was justified and legally in line with (a new understanding of) international law remains alive today. Nevertheless, one fact is clear: since the summer of 1999 and adoption of UNSC Resolution 1244 on 10 June 1999 the reality has changed significantly in Kosovo. *De facto* ruled by the Serbs from 1912 until 1999, the province came under international supervision and became some sort of international protectorate headed by the UN Mission in Kosovo (UNMIK) and aided by other international organisations, including the EU.

3.2.3   The Impact of the War and Conflict Management Activities (1999–2008)

Violence Against Civilians

The war in 1999 produced more than 619,000 refugees, around 700,000 internally displaced people and an international refugee crisis not seen in Europe since World

War II. Almost 2000 people are still listed as missing. By the end of 1999, 820,000 Kosovo Albanians had returned to Kosovo, encountering dangerous landmines and destroyed homes, forcing humanitarian agencies like the United Nations High Commissioner for Refugees to step in and set up rehabilitation programmes (ICMP 2011).

The tide of violence took a new course. As the Kosovo Albanian refugees were returning to their destroyed homeland, many wished to revenge the Serbs living in Kosovo, mostly civilians. Although Kosovo Force (KFOR) troops began arriving, it took some time to establish a basic level of security and safety. Due to this security vacuum, several Kosovo Albanian gangs were formed *ad hoc* and started attacking and intimidating the remaining Serbs and other minority groups. According to some estimates, around 160,000 to 200,000 Serbs and other ethnic minorities left their homes in Kosovo (Glenny 2001, 658–662).

Many have become internally displaced, concentrating in areas with a greater Serbian presence (e.g. Dobratin, Gračanica, Velika Hoča, Goraždevac, Orahovac, Kosovska Mitrovica and other areas north of the Ibar River). Most Serbs killed in this time were unprotected civilians (the FRY troops did not experience such violence as they were both armed and protected by KFOR during the withdrawal from Kosovo). Along with this, several abductions, detentions and different abuses of Serb civilians and other minority groups, including rape, occurred immediately after KFOR troops entered Kosovo; the KLA's intention was to expel from Kosovo all Serbs and other members of ethnic minorities believed to have cooperated with Yugoslav forces before and during the war. A distinctive feature of the armed violence was the systematic destruction of religious heritage, mostly Serb Orthodox sites, after the war in 1999, primarily as part of revenge attacks (Kostadinova 2011).

The Roma, Ashkali, Egyptian and Gorani ethnic minorities were mostly targeted by Albanian paramilitary groups because many Albanians saw them as collaborators with the Serbian side. The population of these communities almost halved compared to the pre-war situation. For example, the Gorani are one of the smallest minorities in Kosovo and only approximately 8000 still live there, whereas almost 18,000 Gorani lived in Kosovo before the war. Data show that the international organisations taking over responsibility for safety and security in Kosovo in June 1999 were anything but effective in preventing violence against non-Albanians (Dursun-Ozkanca 2010).

Building Peace in Kosovo (1999–2008)
Even though the NATO airstrikes were not authorised by the UNSC, they were successful in bringing the mass violence to an end, leading to the FRY troops' withdrawal from Kosovo. Established under UNSC Resolution 1244, UNMIK was *de facto* put in charge of Kosovo and administering it from 10 June 1999 to the declaration of independence in 2008. Its mandate was to establish a functioning civil administration, ensure the overall safety of all ethnic minorities and organise municipal elections (Džihić and Kramer 2009; Yannis 2004, 67).

The mission set up four main pillars to rebuild Kosovo society and prevent new outbreaks of armed conflict. UNMIK was in charge of the first pillar (civil administration), UNHCR of the second pillar (humanitarian assistance), the OSCE was responsible for the third pillar (democratisation and institution-building) and, finally, the EU took on responsibility for the fourth pillar (reconstruction and economic development). In line with UNSCR Resolution 1244, NATO was tasked with maintaining security in Kosovo, meaning the military aspect of peace-building was not included within the framework of the UNMIK civilian mission (Zupančič 2015).

Thus, KFOR troops *de facto* worked as the main security provider, separated from the UNMIK pillar structure. There was much competition and confusion regarding the division of work among all the international actors stationed in Kosovo, even though the division of labour was clearly specified in the four-pillar structure. The first period of UNMIK's presence in Kosovo (1999–2001) was marked by the mentioned mass violence of Kosovo Albanians against Kosovo Serbs and other minorities, which UNMIK and KFOR could not stop due to the small number of experienced staff. The biggest problem had its roots in the mission's mandate since the Special Representative of the Secretary General (SRSG) lacked executive authority over the other missions in Kosovo (Zupančič 2015, 132).

In 2003, UNMIK adopted the so-called Standards for Kosovo, a set of UN-endorsed benchmarks for the development of democracy in Kosovo and an overall improvement in conditions. This came before the start of negotiations on the future status of Kosovo (Knoll 2005, 639). Despite all the efforts to improve the situation and find an agreeable solution to resolve the Kosovar knot, the international organisations were again unable to respond to the outbreak of violent riots in March 2004 when Kosovo Albanians targeted Serb and other ethnic minorities (Weller 2009).

The riots were actually caused by a relatively small incident that triggered a spiral of violence. On 15 March 2004, unknown persons shot and killed an 18-year-old Serb in Čaglavica on the outskirts of Prishtina. Serbs from Čaglavica and the surrounding settlements organised protests and closed off the main road linking Prishtina with the south of Kosovo and Albania immediately following the incident (Zupančič 2015).

Only a day later, three Albanian boys drowned in the Ibar River in unclear circumstances. According to unverified sources, the boys had been chased by a group of Serbs seeking to avenge the murder in Čaglavica. The fact the boys were actually persecuted by the Serbs has not been confirmed by any commission or inquiry. When 'news' of this spread among the Kosovo Albanians, they wanted to cross the bridge in Mitrovica and enter the northern part of the city chiefly populated by Serbs (ibid.).

The planned march against the Serbs was prevented by KFOR. However, violence quickly spread to other parts of Kosovo. After three days of rioting, blood had been spilled: 19 people killed and around 1000 wounded (including 61 members of KFOR and 55 policemen). Moreover, 550 houses and 27 Orthodox churches or monasteries were burned down and over 4000 people—most of Serbian origin—temporarily fled their homes (BBC 2004; Weller 2009, 187).

At first, the March 2004 riots backfired on the Kosovo Albanians as they lost the international community's sympathy which they had enjoyed as the main victims of the armed violence. Yet the riots also served as a wake-up call to the international community indicating the situation in Kosovo was still unstable and the question of Kosovo's political status still had to be resolved (Koeth 2010, 231).

Indeed, after the riots Kai Eide, a special envoy of the UN Secretary-General, prepared a proposal to revise and reconfigure UNMIK. He suggested, among others, that the EU should take on more responsibility for overseeing Kosovo.[15] He also stated the Kosovo Albanians had been dissatisfied with the ineffective international administration. The report continued that new priorities and more realistic standards should be set and negotiations on the status of Kosovo should begin since any delaying of the talks could aggravate the security and political situation. Overall, Kai Eide's report confirmed the situation in Kosovo was unsustainable (Weller 2009, 194–195).

Negotiations started in 2005 when the UN organised talks between Belgrade and Prishtina. On behalf of the UN, the mediation was led by a Finnish diplomat Martti Ahtisaari, who was assisted by officials from the Council of the EU and the European Commission. The chances the talks would find a compromise between the two sides were slim, as "particularly the Serbian politicians feared being associated with a process that would result in a loosening Serbian grip on Kosovo" (WOSCAP 2017, 5).

One year later, the team presented the Comprehensive Status Proposal—the so-called Ahtisaari Plan (Report of the Special Envoy of the Secretary-General on Kosovo's future status 2007).[16] It recommended conditional independence of Kosovo supervised by the international community since reintegration into Serbia was not considered viable but, on the other hand, it was also clear that continuing the international administration was also not sustainable (Koeth 2010, 232; WOSCAP 2017, 5).

In fact, the proposal sought to prepare the grounds for the 'supervised independence' of Kosovo, although the word independence was avoided (Report of the Special Envoy of the Secretary-General on Kosovo's future status 2007). Yet it also provided for extensive rights of the ethnic minorities. This idea was a direct

---

[15]He produced a report on Kosovo's future for UN Secretary-General Kofi Annan. The international community was taken by surprise by the riots in Kosovo in March 2004 and failed to properly understand the depth of dissatisfaction of most of its citizens, as well as the vulnerability of the minority. Moreover, it gave the impression of being in disarray, lacking strategy and internal cohesion. UNMIK became the main target of the criticism, but was in itself a victim of an international policy that lacked cohesion and vision. The report stated that UNMIK needed to be re-energised to bring its various components more closely together and focus on key priorities in a more organised way. However, with the future-status question looming, Eide stated, "UNMIK should be looking to reduce its presence and hand increasing responsibilities to the European Union" (Eide 2004).

[16]*Report of the Special Envoy of the Secretary-General on Kosovo's future status* (Comprehensive proposal for the Kosovo Status Settlement), UN Document S/2007/186.

consequence of the increased cooperation with the OSCE High Commissioner on National Minorities. The proposal included a transition period of 120 days after which the UNMIK mandate would have expired and power would be transferred to Kosovo's governing authorities (Economides and Ker-Lindsay 2010). Ahtisaari's proposal stirred wide debate in the international community. The Kosovo Albanians and NATO endorsed the proposal, while the Kosovo Serbs, the Russian Federation and Serbia all rejected it (Bieber 2015).

Already during the negotiations, the EU started considering Kai Eide's suggestion that the EU play the most prominent role in post-conflict Kosovo society (Eckhart 2016, 92). After all, the EU had by then already established its first police reform mission, as well as a military one in the same region of South East Europe (in Bosnia and Herzegovina). Where, if not in Kosovo, should the EU successfully continue its involvement, was a question that resonated in Brussels; the EU Council was very receptive of such thinking.

In particular, Javier Solana, the EUHR for the CFSP, who had served as NATO Secretary-General during the Kosovo war, saw the EU mission in Kosovo as an important way for the EU to prove itself as a peacebuilding actor (Eckhart 2016, 93). A 2005 report published jointly with Olli Rehn, the EU Commissioner for Enlargement, brought the first official EU statement referring to the future rule-of-law mission in Kosovo. Moreover, in December 2005, when the EU's multi-annual financial framework (2007–2013) was being discussed, the budget for CSDP missions and operations turned out to be substantially higher than previously anticipated (ibid.).

Already in January 2006, the EU dispatched a joint Council-Commission Fact Finding Mission to Kosovo to explore the scope of action of any possible EU mission in the field of the rule of law. The Fact Finding Mission recommended the EU set up a planning team to prepare a possible rule-of-law mission integrating the police, justice and customs dimensions. An EU Planning Team (EUPT) was therefore established in April of the same year. The EU's member states and institutions based their approach on the expectation the negotiations on Kosovo's future status would end by late 2006 or early 2007. The EUPT included 80 international and 55 local personnel. It had a justice, police and administration team and was mandated to "initiate planning to ensure a smooth transition between selected tasks of UNMIK and a possible ESDP operation" (Grevi 2009, 356).

Initially, three modes of deployment were discussed: light, medium and robust, with light being the preferred option since the EU was still hoping for a UN solution. The light option meant the deployment of no more than 850 experts who would monitor and advise local officials; the medium option meant more staff who would focus on a stronger police and customs component, made up of 800 to 900 international personnel; while the robust option implied substantially greater staff and more extensive executive powers. The planning mission also based its functioning on the assumption any mission would focus more on the tasks of monitoring, mentoring and advising (MMA), and limit its executive powers to a minimum. The objective would be to transfer ownership as soon as possible to the local authorities, putting them in the driver's seat (Grevi 2009, 357).

However, despite the vague intention to use the EU's conflict-prevention instruments in Kosovo, the EU remained politically divided on the issue of the Ahtisaari Plan and the question of Kosovo's future political status. While 22 states accepted the proposal, 5 expressed reservations (Cyprus, Greece, Romania, Slovakia and Spain). Romania and Slovakia were officially against due to, as they argued, the lack of legitimacy since the UNSC had not approved it. Cyprus, Greece and Spain were more worried about the situation in their own countries: Spain had been fighting secessionist movements in its territory for decades (Basque, Catalonia), and Cyprus and Greece still had unresolved issues with the Turkish community on Cyprus (Tzifakis 2013). One group of states insisted the UNSC should have passed a legally binding resolution based on the Ahtisaari proposals, while those opposed to the proposal suggested new negotiations. It was soon obvious that a unanimous solution could not be reached within the UNSC (Richter 2009).

Seeing that no solution would come from the UNSC, the UN Secretary-General formed what is called the Troika. The Troika consisted of experienced diplomats from the most relevant international actors: Frank Wisner (the USA), Wolfgang Ischinger (the EU) and Alexander Botsan-Kharchenko (the Russian Federation). The three diplomats were tasked with facilitating a further round of negotiations to last 120 days, starting in August 2007. They were supported by all parties to the conflict, as well as the Russian Federation, the USA, the EU, NATO and the UN. The Troika reaffirmed that the UNSC resolutions, the Guiding principles of the Contact Group and the Ahtisaari Plan should be the basis for settling the status issue. However, the Troika clearly stated it would gladly accept any other alternative solution if agreed to by all parties to the conflict (ibid.).

Their work was carried out over 10 sessions, 6 of which were face-to-face dialogues, including a final 3-day conference in Austria, and 2 trips to the region. During the negotiations the two sides insisted on their demands: the Kosovo Albanians demanded independence based on the Ahtisaari Plan, while the Serbs rejected it. Despite the Troika's innovative suggestions, neither side was prepared to yield. It is also important to note that during the negotiations the local population in Kosovo felt extremely frustrated since they were not included in the talks regarding the very place they were living in and the future that awaited them (Caruso 2008; Zupančič 2015).

The key conclusion of the Troika was that no agreeable solution could be found and that any further negotiations would be futile. After this message was brought to the UN, the UNSC signalled it was giving up on trying to find a negotiated solution, and that any further work on the issue should come from the outside the UN. In these circumstances, the EU, backed by the USA, stepped in. European and American representatives announced their intention to take over the responsibility, while Moscow clearly reiterated that any acceptable solution should have the UNSC's backing (Caruso 2008). The stage was thus set for the EU to demonstrate its capacities and power as a global and regional peacebuilding actor ('a force for good'), able to project its normative standards on the external environment.

References

Andreatta, F. (1997). The Bosnian war and the new world order failure and success of international intervention. Occasional paper, Institute for security studies Western European Union. Retrieved October 21, 2017, from https://www.peacepalacelibrary.nl/ebooks/files/occ01.pdf.

BBC. (2004). Kosovo clashes 'ethnic cleansing'. Retrieved December 12, 2017, from http://news.bbc.co.uk/2/hi/europe/3551571.stm.

Becker, J. (2017). In the Yugoslav mirror: the EU disintegration crisis. *Globalizations, 14*(6), 840–850.

Bekaj, A. R. (2010). *The KLA and the Kosovo war. From intra-state conflict to independent country.* Berlin: Berghof Conflict Research.

Bellamy, A. J. (2008). The responsibility to protect and the problem of military intervention. *International Affairs, 84*(4), 615–639.

Bieber, F. (2015). The Serbia-Kosovo agreements: an EU success story? *Review of Central and East European Law, 40,* 285–319.

Boer, N. den, & Borgh, C. van den. (2011). International statebuilding and contentious universities in Kosovo. *Journal of Intervention and Statebuilding, 5*(1), 67–88.

Borgh, C. van der (2012). Resisting international state building in Kosovo. *Problems of Post-Communism, 59*(2), 31–42.

Brenner, M. (1992). The EC in Yugoslavia: A debut performance. *Security Studies, 1*(4), 586–609.

Caruso, U. (2008). Kosovo declaration of independence and international community—An assessment by the Kosovo monitoring task force. *JEMIE, 7*(2).

Ćorović, V. (1993). Istorija srpskog naroda. Internetna izdaja. Beograd: BIGZ. Retrieved December 13, 2017, from http://www.svetlost.org/podaci/coroviceva_istorija_srba.pdf.

Daskalovski, Ž. (2003). Claims to Kosovo: nationalism and self-determination. In F. Bieber & Ž. Daskalovski (Eds.), *Understanding the war in Kosovo.* London: Routledge.

Djeković, L. (1989). Privredna kriza i privredna reforma u Jugoslaviji. In M. Korošič (Ed.), *Quo vadis, Jugoslavijo?* (pp. 23–40). Zagreb: Naprijed.

Dolenc, D., Baketa, N., & Maassen, P. (2014). Europeanizing higher education and research systems of the Western Balkans. In J. Braković, P. Maassen, B. Stensaker, & M. Vukasović (Eds.), *The re-institutionalization of higher education in the Western Balkans* (pp. 61–91). Frankfurt a. M.: Lang.

Drançolli, J. (1984). Albanci v srednjem veku. In J. Stanič (Ed.), *Albanci* (pp. 25–35). Ljubljana: Cankarjeva založba.

Drançolli, J. (2008). Illyrian-Albanian continuity on the area of Kosova. *Thesis Kosova, 1*(1), 29–46.

Dranqoli, A. (2011). Tito's attempt to integrate Albania into Yugoslavia, 1945–1948. *History studies, 3*(2), 191–196.

Duchêne, F. (1973). The EC and the uncertainties of interdependence. In M. Kohnstamm & W. Hager (Eds.), *A nation writ large? Foreign policy problems before the EC.* London: Macmillan.

Dursun-Ozkanca, O. (2010). Does it take four to tango? A comparative analysis of international collaboration on peacebuilding in Bosnia and Herzegovina and Kosovo. *Journal of Balkan and Near Eastern studies, 12*(4), 437–456. Retrieved December 12, 2017, from http://www.tandfonline.com/doi/pdf/10.1080/19448953.2010.531213?needAccess=true.

Džihić, V., & Kramer H. (2009). Kosovo after independence. Is the EU's EULEX mission delivering on its promises? Retrieved April 16, 2017, from http://library.fes.de/pdf-files/id/ipa/06571.pdf.

Eckhard, S. (2016). *International assistance to police reform: managing peacebuilding.* London: Palgrave Macmillan.

Economides, S., & Ker-Lindsay, J. (2010). Forging EU foreign policy unity from diversity: The 'unique case' of the Kosovo status talks. *European Foreign Affairs Review, 15,* 495–510.

Eide, K. (2004). Kosovo: The way forward. Retrieved October 29, 2017, from https://www.nato.int/cps/en/natohq/opinions_21120.htm?selectedLocale=en.

Elsie, R. (2017). Vaso Cubrilovic: The expulsion of the Albanians—Memorandum. Retrieved December 12, 2017, from http://albanianhistory.net/1937_Cubrilovic/index.html.

Ginsberg, R. H. (1989). *Foreign policy actions of the EC: the politics of scale*. Boulder: Lynne Rienner.

Ginsberg, R. H. (2001). *The European Union in international politics: Baptism by fire*. Lanham: Rowman & Littlefield Publishers Inc.

Glaurdić, J. (2011). *The hour of Europe: Western powers and the breakup of Yugoslavia*. New Haven: Yale University Press.

Glenny, M. (2001). *The Balkans 1804–1999: Nationalism, war and the great powers*. London: Penguin.

Grevi, G. (2009). The EU rule-of-law mission in Kosovo. In G. Grevi, D. Helly, & D. Keohane (Eds.), *European security and defense policy: The first ten years (1999–2009)* (pp. 353–368). Paris: The European Union Institute for Security Studies.

Helsinki Committee for Human Rights in Serbia. (2016). International Community and the Balkan Wars. Retrieved October 22, 2017, from www.helsinki.org.rs/doc/int%20community.doc.

Hoxha, H. (1984). Kosovo in Albanci v novi Jugoslaviji. In J. Stanič (Ed.), *Albanci* (pp. 201–226). Ljubljana: Cankarjeva založba.

ICMP. 2011. "ICMP issues report on persons missing from the Kosovo conflict". Retrieved January 8, 2018, from http://www.icmp.int/press-releases/kosovo-stock-taking-report/.

Islami, H. (1994). *Demographic Reality in Kosovo*. Priština: Academy of Sciences and Arts & Kosova, Kosova Information Center.

Jelavich, B. (1983). *History of the Balkans: Twentieth century*. Cambridge: Cambridge University Press.

Joseph, E. P. (2005). Back to the Balkans. *Foreign Affairs, 84*(1), 111–122.

Judah, T. (2002). *Kosovo: War and revenge*. New Haven: Yale University Press.

Juncos, A. (2005). The EU's post-conflict intervention in Bosnia and Herzegovina: Re(integrating) the Balkans and/or (re)inventing the EU? *Southeast European Politics, 6*(2), 88–108.

Keukeleire, S., & MacNaughtan, J. (2008). *The foreign policy of the European Union*. New York: Palgrave Macmillan.

King, I., & Mason, W. (2006). *Peace at any price: How the world failed in Kosovo*. London: Cornell University Press.

Knoll, B. (2005). From Benchmarking to Final Status? Kosovo and the Problem of an International Administration's Open-Ended Mandate. *The European Journal of International Law, 16*(4), 637–660.

Koeth, W. (2010). State building without a state: the EU's dilemma in defining its relations with Kosovo. *European Foreign Affairs Review, 15*, 227–247.

Kostadinova, T. (2011). Cultural diplomacy in war-affected societies: International and local policies in the post-conflict (re)construction of religious heritage in former Yugoslavia. Retrieved January 8, 2018, from http://www.culturaldiplomacy.org/academy/content/pdf/participant-papers/academy/Tonka-Kostadinova-Cultural-diplomacy-in-war-affected-societies.pdf.

Krstić, B. (2006). *Kosovo: Facing the court of history*. New York: Humanity Books.

Kubo, K. (2010). Why Kosovar Albanians took up arms against the Serbian regime: The genesis and expansion of the UÇK in Kosovo. *Europe-Asia Studies, 62*(7), 1135–1152.

Lampe, J. R. (1996). Yugoslavia in History: Twice there was a Country. Cambridge: Cambridge University Press.

Lindstrom, N. (2003). Between Europe and the Balkans: Mapping Slovenia and Croatia's return to Europe in the 1990s. *Dialectical Anthropology, 27*, 313–329.

Mahmutćehajić, R. (2001). The road to war. In B. Magaš & I. Žanić (Eds.), *The war in Croatia and Bosnia-Herzegovina* (pp. 1991–1995). London: Frank Cass.

Malcolm, N. (1999). *Kosovo: A short history*. New York: University Press, New York.

Meier, V. (2005). *A history of its demise*. London: Routledge.

Mertus, J. (1999). *Kosovo: How myths and truths started a war.* Berkeley: University of California Press.

Mulaj, K. (2008). Resisting an oppressive regime: the case of Kosovo Liberation Army. *Studies in Conflict & Terrorism, 31*(12), 1103–1119.

Nečak, D. (1984). Kosovo med NOB. In J. Stanič (Ed.), *Albanci* (pp. 187–200). Ljubljana: Cankarjeva založba.

New York Times. (1991). Conflict in Yugoslavia; Europeans send high-level team. Retrieved October 21, 2017, from http://www.nytimes.com/1991/06/29/world/conflict-in-yugoslavia-europeans-send-high-level-team.html.

Pearson, O. (2006). *Albania in the twentieth century, a history: Volume II: Albania in occupation and war, 1939–45.* London: I. B. Tauris.

Pilegaard, J. (2004). The European Security and Defence Policy and the development of a security strategy for Europe. In J. Pilegaard (Ed.), *The politics of European security.* Copenhagen: Danish Institute for International Studies.

Popović, M. V. (1976). *Vidovdan i časni krst.* Beograd: Slovo ljubve.

Radan, P. (2000). Post-secession international borders: A critical analysis of the opinions of the Badinter Arbitration Commission. *Melbourne University Law Review, 50*(24).

Radio Free Europe. (1983). Aleksandar Rankovic—political profile of a Yugoslav »Stalinist« . RAD Background Report/205 (Yugoslavia). Retrieved December 21, 2017, from http://storage.osaarchivum.org/low/d2/31/d23199e2-bcc2–4981-82fc-d4f28fa64dfd_l.pdf.

Report of the Special Envoy of the Secretary-General on Kosovo's future status (Comprehensive proposal for the Kosovo Status Settlement). (2007). UN Document S/2007/186. Retrieved January 8, 2018, from https://www.kuvendikosoves.org/common/docs/Comprehensive%20Proposal%20.pdf.

Richter, S. (2009). Promoting rule of law without state-building: Can EULEX square the circle in Kosovo? In M. Asseburg & R. Kempin (Eds.), *The EU as a strategic actor in the realm of security and defence? A systematic assessment of ESDP missions and operations* (pp. 30–45). Berlin: German Institute for International and Security Affairs.

Rogel, C. (2003). Kosovo: Where it all began. *International Journal of Politics, Culture, and Society, 17*(1), 167–182.

Rrecaj, B. (2006). *The right to self-determination and statehood: The case of Kosovo.* Buffalo: University of Buffalo.

Rusinow, D. (2008). *Yugoslavia: Oblique insights and observations.* Pittsburgh: University of Pittsburgh.

Ruvarac, I. (1992). O knezu Lazaru. In R. Mihaljčič (Ed.), *Boj na Kosovu, starija i novija saznanja (The battle odd Kosovo, older and more recent discoveries).* Književne novine: Beograd.

Simić, P. (2000). *Put u Rambuje: Kosovska kriza 1995–2000.* Belgrade: Nea.

Skendi, S. (1953). Beginnings of Albanian nationalist and autonomous trends: The Albanian League, 1878–1881. *The American Slavic and East European Review, 12*(2), 219–232.

Sontag, S. (2003). *Regarding the pain of others.* New York: Farrar, Straus & Giroux.

Srpska akademija nauka i umetnosti. (1986). *Memorandum Srpske akademije znanosti i umetnosti (nacrt).* Beograd: Srpska akademija nauka i umetnosti. Retrieved December 21, 2017, from http://www.helsinki.org.rs/serbian/doc/memorandum%20sanu.pdf.

Stanič, J. (1984). Albanija Enverja Hoxhe. In J. Stanič (Ed.), *Albanci* (pp. 145–163). Ljubljana: Cankarjeva založba.

Surroi, V. (1997). Mehrheit und Minderheit in Kosovo: Albaner contra Serben. *Internationale Politik, 52*(10), 49–52.

Sweeney, J., Holsoe J., Vulliamy E. (1999). NATO bombed Chinese deliberately. The Observer. Retrieved November 8, 2017, from http://www.guardian.co.uk/world/1999/oct/17/Balkans.

Todorova, M. (2001). *Imaginarij Balkana.* Ljubljana: Inštitut za civilizacijo. in kulturo.

Tzifakis, N. (2013). The European Union in Kosovo, reflecting on the credibility and efficiency deficit. *Problems of Post-Communism, 60*(1), 43–54.

Uvalic, M. (1997). European Economic Integration: What Role for the Balkans? In S. Bianchini and M. Uvalic (Eds.), *The balkans and the challenge of economic integration: regional and european perspectives* (pp. 19–34). Ravenna: Longo Editore.

Vickers, M. (1997). *The Albanians: A modern history*. New York: Tauris.

Voje, I. (1994). *Nemirni Balkan: zgodovinski pregled od 6. do 18. stoletja*. Ljubljana: DZS.

Watkins, C. (2003). *The Balkans*. New York: Nova Publishers.

Weller, M. (2009). *Contested statehood: Kosovo's struggle for independence*. New York: Kosovo University Press.

Woodward, S. L. (1995). *Balkan tragedy: Chaos and dissolution after the cold war*. Washington, D.C.: Brookings Institution.

WOSCAP. (2017). EU peacebuilding capabilities in Kosovo after 2008: An analysis of EULEX and the EU-facilitated Belgrade-Prishtina Dialogue. Part A of Deliverable 3.1: Desk Review Case Studies. Retrieved November 16, 2017, from http://www.woscap.eu/documents/131298403/131299900/Kosovo+report_PU+%285%29.pdf/3f0fb0f7-e81c-4e42-bdee-c43efabfafed.

Wouters, J., & Naert, F. (2004). The EU and conflict prevention: A brief historic overview. In V. Kronenberger & J. Wouters (Eds.), *The European Union and conflict prevention: Policy and legal aspects*. Asser: Haag.

Yannis, A. (2004). The UN as government in Kosovo. *Global Governance, 10*(1), 67–81.

Zupančič, R. (2015). *Kosovo: laboratorij preprečevanja oboroženih konfliktov, pokonfliktne obnove in izgradnje države*. Brno: Vaclav Klemm in Plzen: Zapadočeska univerzita v Plzni.

Zupančič, R. (2016). Preprečevanje, prepričevanje, obžalovanje: ZDA, razpad SFRJ in diplomatsko (ne)priznanje neodvisnosti in samostojnosti Republike Slovenije (1990–1992). *Teorija in Praksa, 53*(2), 312–344.

Zupančič, R., & Arbeiter, J. (2016). 'Primitive, cruel and blood-thirsty savages': Stereotypes in and about the Western Balkans. *Teorija in Praksa, 53*(5), 1051–1063.

Chapter 4
EULEX Kosovo: Projecting the EU's Normative Power via a Rule-of-Law Mission

EULEX Kosovo was deployed in very difficult political conditions. Already on 14 December 2007, the European Council had approved the mission's sending of 1800 to 1900 people to Kosovo. The final decision on the deployment of EULEX was planned to be taken on 28 January 2008. However, it was postponed due to concerns over the EU lacking the legal grounds for the deployment and the problem of Kosovo's unresolved political status that were raised by particular member states (Grevi 2009, 354–355). At the time, the media speculated the delay was due to the EU's concerns over the second round of the presidential elections in Serbia taking place on 3 February 2008, as well as the possibility of signing the Stabilisation and Association Agreement with Serbia on the same day. These rumours were denied by EU sources (B92 2008).

On 4 February 2008, the EU Council adopted a joint action establishing the mission (Council Joint Action 2008a) and appointed Dutch diplomat Pieter Feith as the EUSR in Kosovo (Council Joint Action 2008b). The final decision to deploy the mission was, however, made as late as 16 February 2008 (External Relations Council 2008). The mission's task was to support the Kosovar authorities in all areas related to the rule of law, with priorities including to address immediate concerns regarding the protection of minority communities, corruption and the fight against organised crime (Grevi 2009).

Kosovo declared its independence only one day later, on 17 February 2008, and committed itself to implementing the Ahtisaari Plan (van der Borgh 2012). By substituting UNMIK with its own mission, the EU wanted to take over the political ownership and oversight of the process of Kosovo's independence, which could not happen without a compromise among EU member states. The day after the declaration of independence, the Council noted the EU member states would accept their decisions on their relations with Kosovo in line with national practice and international law (Zupančič and Udovič 2011).

In short, "while consensus could be achieved within the Union to launch an ESDP operation mandated to reform and support Kosovo's rule of law institutions, member states diverged on the recognition of Kosovo as an independent state" (Grevi 2009, 356). The mission was therefore framed as having a neutral status and retaining

© The Author(s) 2018
R. Zupančič and N. Pejič, *Limits to the European Union's Normative Power in a Post-conflict Society*, SpringerBriefs in Population Studies,
https://doi.org/10.1007/978-3-319-77824-2_4

executive powers combined with a widespread local presence. It was argued that the mission's neutral status was a consequence of an innovative procedure within the EU whereby member states put their disagreements aside and instead discussed those points they could all agree on (Interview 7 2016f and 9 2016h).

However, some of those interviewed as part of our project go further and claim that EULEX's creation was an excuse for the lack of any clear policy and commitment to Kosovo of the non-recognising countries and the EU as a whole, while trying to showcase the EU's strong position within the region. This absence of any clear policy and commitment was masked by the emphasis on more technical aspects of the police reform and, as will be shown in this chapter, has posed a significant obstacle to EULEX's performance in Kosovo. As Radin (2014, 183) puts it, EULEX has been in the "awkward position of assisting the Kosovo government while having no formal opinion about whether Kosovo was an autonomous region of Serbia or an independent state".

Mandate

Nonetheless, political ambiguity did not stop the EU member states deploying the first EULEX officers, which then amounted to fewer than 500 personnel (or about one-quarter of the planned figure). De Wet (2009) emphasises that in the transition period EULEX had to accept some compromises regarding its functioning; the postponing of the final negotiation phase regarding the status by one year, as well as the drastic end to the negotiations with Kosovo's unilateral declaration of independence in February 2008, altered many of the original assumptions.

The first of these assumptions was that EULEX would take over reform of the security sector and institution-building in the area of the rule of law, as envisaged in the Ahtisaari Plan. The Ahtisaari Plan had proposed a transition period of 120 days for the Kosovo Assembly to adopt the Constitution and relevant legislation in compliance with the proposal. But the Plan itself remained disputed at the international level while Kosovo Serb municipalities also rejected the proposed legislation.

Second, EULEX was not in a position to be deployed all across Kosovo. North of the Ibar River, Kosovo Serbs demonstrated opened resistance. In 2011, they demolished two crossing points linking Kosovo to central Serbia (Jarinje and Brnjak). Three years earlier, in March 2008, a group of Serbs occupied the court building in northern Mitrovica. Such actions made customs collection and the exercise of jurisdiction in the north of Kosovo temporary impossible. Moreover, Serb-majority municipalities in northern Kosovo (Kosovska Mitrovica, Leposavić, Zvečan and Zubin Potok) several times participated in Serbian parliamentary and local elections, electing new city councils outside of the Kosovo state jurisdiction.

Third, there was considerable confusion regarding which law applied to the police, judiciary and customs services—Kosovo Serb authorities in the north of Kosovo applied the 'UNMIK law' (adopted between 1999 and 2007) or earlier Yugoslav regulations, while the new Kosovar authorities enforced new legislation that was meant to be applied all over the country (Grevi 2009, 356–357).

Next, the expected transfer of authority and equipment (buildings, vehicles) from UNMIK to EULEX did not happen since the two missions still co-existed side by side in 2009. UNMIK was unable to scale down as quickly as anticipated, while EULEX was unable to deploy according to the planned schedule—both factors caused uncomfortable friction between the missions (Grevi 2009, 357). Facing the dilemma of whether to deploy only in parts of Kosovo (Albanian majority areas), with the risk of paving the way towards the eventual split of the country along ethnic lines, or to wait for an improvement of the political context to deploy Kosovo-wide, EULEX entered a period of operational hibernation until December 2009, when EULEX's initial operational capability was finally declared (Grevi 2009, 359). During that transition period, the Head of the EULEX mission delegated the responsibility to undertake the activities necessary for EULEX to be fully operational to EUPT (WOSCAP 2017).

Finally, the political impasse complicated the position of the International Civilian Representative (ICR)/EUSR and complicated its relations with EULEX. The first problem already appeared in the role of the EUSR. Shortly after independence, Peter Feith was appointed the first ICR in Kosovo by the International Steering Group (a group of countries that recognised Kosovo's independence and supported full implementation of the Ahtisaari Plan from the outset).

Peter Feith then had two duties to perform; one as the EUSR and the other as the ICR. As the WOSCAP report (2017, 21) notes "when performing his ICR tasks, Feith had to constantly declare the irreversibility and importance of Kosovo's newly gained independence for stability in the region, while as the EUSR he represented the EU—of which five countries did not recognize Kosovo's independence". According to Greiçevci (2011, 297), this has hindered EULEX's capacity to act as a consistent actor in Kosovo. Moreover, it has created a problem in planning the mission's activities. For example, the Greeks and the Cypriots argued there could be no reference to specific Kosovar ministries as a counterpart to EULEX in any EULEX documents since that would per se imply that Kosovo is an independent state (WOSCAP 2017, 21).

The EULEX mission has therefore been unique in many respects. Its mandate, adopted in February 2008, is vast and unprecedented in the context of the civilian CSDP. When launched, the mission's main goal was to support and assist local institutions, judicial authorities and law enforcement agencies in becoming accountable, inter-ethnic, sustainable and independent of political interference, according to the best international and so-called European standards (Grevi 2009, 356–357).

As declared in Article 2 of the Council Joint Action (2008a), the mandate of the EULEX is to:

assist the Kosovo institutions, judicial authorities and law enforcement agencies in their progress towards sustainability and accountability and in further developing and strengthening an independent multi-ethnic justice system and multi-ethnic police and customs service, ensuring that these institutions are free from political interference and adhering to internationally recognised standards and European best practices. EULEX KOSOVO, in full cooperation with the European Commission Assistance Programmes, shall fulfil its mandate through monitoring, mentoring and advising, while retaining certain executive responsibilities.

The first mandate of EULEX from 2008 until 2010 was therefore supporting Kosovar authorities by MMA activities in each rule-of-law component (judiciary, police, customs). Through these activities, EULEX was assisting Kosovar institutions, judicial authorities and law enforcement agencies so as to reinforce a multi-ethnic justice system, police, and customs service.

In addition, EULEX obtained *executive powers*. Those functions were "narrower in scope, covering the repression and prevention of crime, civil justice and crowd and riot control" (Capussela 2015, 107). They were also residual in nature, meaning that EULEX only exercises them when its MMA activities were insufficient. In those cases, EULEX had a duty to act. Particularly in criminal matters, the mission's task was to ensure that cases of war crimes, terrorism, organised crime, corruption, inter-ethnic crimes, financial/economic crimes and other serious crimes are properly investigated and prosecuted (European Union External Action 2015).

The criteria for deciding to act in an executive or advisory capacity were set in the mission's operational plan, as well as in Kosovar law, according to which "the mission's police and judicial staff must investigate, prosecute and judge the cases that fall into a set of pre-defined categories—which Kosovo's authorities were *ex ante* deemed not yet fit to deal with—as well as those lesser crimes in respect of which the domestic authorities appeared unable or unwilling to act impartially and effectively" (Capussela 2015, 107). With regard to such executive powers, Capussela (ibid.) notes that EULEX's mandate was daunting, especially considering how "widespread crime and impunity were in Kosovo and how weak its law enforcement system was".

To fulfil these tasks, EULEX was allocated an annual budget of approximately EUR 125 million and a staff exceeding 3000 during the first four years of its functioning until 2012 (EULEX 2016a). For comparison, in early 2008 UNMIK had a budget of EUR 160 million and a staff of approximately 5000, although the UN mission was not only in charge of the rule of law but also of administering Kosovo (Capussela 2015, 108). In June 2010, EULEX's mandate was prolonged by another two years. Content-wise, another extension of EULEX's mandate came in 2012 when the mission was reconfigured into two major sections: the Executive Division, focused on the mission's executive mandate, and the 'Strengthening Division' aimed at working on MMA activities in the local judiciary, customs and police (EULEX 2016a; Fig. 4.1).

In addition to these two core objectives, another two operational objectives of EULEX should be mentioned. Through its 'North' objective, the Mission sought to restore the rule of law throughout the north of Kosovo (areas north of the Ibar River mostly populated by the Serbs). In this regard, EULEX maintained its executive functions at the Mitrovica Basic Court and provided structured MMA support to the key leadership of Kosovo Regional Command North.

The fourth operational objective of EULEX's mandate was supporting the implementation of dialogue between Serbia and Kosovo. In practice, this meant the mission was obliged to provide technical support in implementing rule-of-law related agreements reached in the EU-facilitated dialogue, including the integration of Kosovo Serbs into Kosovar security structures and some other tasks (EULEX 2016a).

Fig. 4.1 Two sides of EULEX's mandate (IECEU 2016b)

In the second half of 2012, the number of authorised staff was reduced to 1250 'internationals' and 1000 positions for local support staff (Capussela 2015, 114). The next important change in the mission's mandate came on 12 June 2014 when the EULEX's mandate was again redefined (Council Decision 2014/349 CFSP). A new composition of the court panels was set. Since then, the composition has consisted of a majority from Kosovo, with 'internationals' being in the minority.

Further, it was decided that EULEX would not take on new cases and would gradually hand over competences to the Kosovar judicial system, with the exception of Northern Kosovo where EULEX was supposed to remain in charge of judicial proceedings until the EU Facilitated Dialogue between Serbia and Kosovo also brought a solution for the judiciary (ibid.). In June 2016, the Council of EU extended the mission's mandate until June 2018 and provided over EUR 60 million for the mission's budget. This prolongation of the mandate for another two years did not bring any substantial changes and followed the path of handing over responsibilities to the Kosovar authorities (Boštjančič Pulko and Pejič 2016, 111; Zupančič et al. 2017).

The EULEX mission is therefore complex and its mandate is constantly evolving and integrating new challenges needing to be addressed by the mission. It is moreover challenged by public opinion in Kosovo. This CSDP mission attracts broad and often legitimate criticism of deficiencies in the planning and implementation of the mission's mandate, including criticism from its own personnel; further, it is often criticised in academic circles (Greiçevci 2011; Radin 2014; Qehaja 2017; Mahr 2017; Zupančič et al. 2017). We can briefly point to the so-called Jacque Report published in April 2015, published in answer to public accusations by a mission staff member who highlighted the existence of corruption in the judiciary (Jacque 2015).

Federica Mogherini, the EUHR for CFSP, wanted to clarify these allegations. She asked Professor Jean-Paul Jacque to investigate them. In his report, Jacque refuted the concrete allegations of corruption, but also highlighted important shortcomings of the EULEX mission. In doing so, he proposed this CSDP mission be completely reformed, or consider a complete withdrawal from Kosovo (Jacque 2015).

Dr Andrea Capussela, another former worker at the mission, not only thinks the mission is unsuccessful in fulfilling its mandate; its presence is even hurting Kosovo, hence EULEX should be recalled immediately (Capussela 2015). Kursani (2013), Radin (2014), Malešič and Juvan (2015) also note the mission has only made limited progress with the judiciary, especially in relation to organised crime and corruption. Moreover, the 2012 European Court of Auditors report found the EU assistance to Kosovo has not been sufficiently effective in relation to the rule of law, once again notably in terms of the pervasiveness of corruption and organised crime (The European Court of Auditors 2012).

However, it is indeed not surprising that the peacebuilding literature often examines Kosovo as a case study since it is the largest and longest running civilian CSDP mission ever deployed by the EU (Grilj and Zupančič 2016). Therefore, a theme in the literature is to regard EULEX Kosovo as a case study of the constantly evolving CSDP (Kammel 2011; Grilj and Zupančič 2016).

The following subchapters will take a different and innovative approach in identifying the limits of the EULEX mission. In accordance with the book's theoretical framework, we explore whether the EU is expressing its normative identity in its interactions with others—does it see it as its obligation to contribute to peace, does it build its image as a peacebuilding actor. It will analyse if the EU's normative interests are others-empowering, based on values perceived as a force for good, which reflect the mission's ultimate goals (in our case, peacebuilding). Moreover, it will assess whether the EU itself 'behaves' according to the values and norms it itself promotes, and if it tries to reproduce these norms elsewhere. Last but not least, the normative ends achieved with this—which we will consider thoroughly—should also be a force for good. The outcomes of the mission should be to correct the attitudes and behaviours in 'a targeted country' that once led to violent conflict.

4.1 Police

With regard to strengthening the Kosovo Police, EULEX has specifically wanted to pursue a strategic approach. Previously, the UNMIK mission included a large international policing component (UNMIK Police) with two tasks: to establish a new police force and maintain civil law and order. However, as noted by Eckhard (2016, 102), EULEX mission "managers were determined not to repeat what they perceived as a mistake made by UNMIK"—before then, the international community's involvement "had been considered as extremely reactive to the immediate necessities on the ground, lacking strategic over- and fore-sight" (Spernbauer 2010, 18).

As a result, the mission's administration ('Programme Office') drafted the so-called programmatic approach that outlined a cascade of activities in the Programme Implementation Documents (PIDs) (EULEX 2009, 6). These included a list of MMA activities. For example, one action aimed to formulate a crime-reduction strategy together with the Kosovo police. Each of these actions was linked to performance indicators and a scheme that enabled reporting.[1] In short, the document was there to ensure that concrete outputs on the ground would follow the mission's strategic objectives (Eckhard 2016, 102).[2]

In the EULEX's own wording, what is envisaged in the document "is a process of reform: i.e. moving Kosovo's police /.../ from their 'current state' to a 'desirable state' of sustainability, accountability, multi-ethnicity, freedom from political interference, and adherence to internationally recognised standards and European best practices" (EULEX 2009, 7). This statement clearly refers to the EU's normative identity in this case of peacebuilding: the desirable state is what the EU perceives as its contribution to peace in the country (if the desirable state is ever achieved). The EU is therefore setting a 'standard' or a normative interest of its foreign policy that is empowering somebody other than itself, it is a statement of values. It reflects the 'good' goals of peacebuilding: "the 'desired end state' envisages rule of law institutions that are able to operate without international intervention or substitution" (EULEX 2009, 7).

In the next few years, 11 Project Implementation Documents were produced, focussing the MMA actions on four main areas according to the 'baseline assessment' established in June 2009 that presented the shortcomings of the Kosovar police force (EULEX 2009, 12). In the documents following the baseline assessment, these four key action areas were tackling criminal activities more effectively, conducting effective patrolling and ensuring public order, providing secure borders and, lastly, strategic policing and management. Another important action was to keep the Kosovar police as multi-ethnic as possible, with a considerable share of Serbs being integrated into the police force.

Some capabilities were to be established from scratch, such as the protection of sites and monuments of religious nature, a border police along 'the green border' with Macedonia and a task force to deal with corruption (EULEX 2010, 4). According to EULEX's own reports, there was almost always progress in each of these four key areas. In a report noting progress between 2009 and 2010, for example, three out of the four areas are graded with a B (slow progress/need more impetus), while "providing secure borders" is ranked as A (progress) (EULEX Programme Report 2010, 7). This shows the EU itself believes it is achieving the normative peacebuilding goals, indeed improving the circumstances required to achieve a peaceful society (addressing 'bad' behaviour). However, is this really the case?

Despite the initial EUPT findings that the main focus of EULEX should be the judicial sector, the initial deployment of EULEX personnel looked more like a robust executive police mission (in its structure and staff composition) than a

---

[1]EULEX based its self-assessment on EULEX monitors dispersed throughout the police component over a period of time. For more details, see the CONOPS and related documents referring to PIDs, as the instruments whereby programme activities, performance indicators and reporting mechanisms are defined (EULEX 2009, 9).

[2]A 'catalogue' of all MMA Actions can be found at the EULEX official website: http://www.eulex-kosovo.eu/en/tracking/.

judiciary (Interview 18 2016p). While some interviewees suggested there might be financial reasons behind it, noting judges and judicial staff are much more expensive than police, others claim this was a necessary first step to secure basic conditions for development of the rule of law (Interview 9 2016h).

4.1.1 Security Environment

Although the mission was deployed to Kosovo almost one decade after the end of major armed hostilities, several interviewees mentioned the issue of security limitations due to security threats. EULEX employees pointed out that "it took almost a year for Head of Mission to sign permission for EULEX police to go on joint patrols with Kosovo Police in the North, and even that was limited only to daytime" (Interview 14 2016l).

This has prevented the mission from realising its objective of strengthening the rule of law. On numerous occasions, Kosovo Serbs have erected barricades and roadblocks in the North of Kosovo that effectively prevented EULEX, as well as Kosovar Customs and Police, from operating north of the Ibar River and thus reaching Kosovo's northern border with Serbia. Protests and resistance in the north have probably also had an impact on the reluctance to engage EULEX more in the north (in order not to provoke more riots and violence) (Interview 7 2016f). Such limits have had a negative impact on the wider picture of the mission's engagements, and thus also resulted in reduced efficiency, especially in its executive mandate (Mahr 2017; Qehaja and Prezelj 2017). These concerns were strengthened in 2013 when EULEX suffered a tremendous blow when its Lithuanian customs officer Audrius Senavicius was shot and killed in his car near Zvečan north of the Ibar (Interview 20 2016r).

It should be noted that EULEX's inability to access northern Kosovo has decreased in the last couple of years; some positive changes have been made for the movement and security of EULEX staff in northern Kosovo, although access is still not as good as in areas south of the Ibar River (Cierco and Reis 2014). The failure to also ensure a comprehensive presence in the north was exposed as an important EULEX shortcoming (Interview 11 2016j). Security limitations thus remain one of the main factors seriously constraining any greater executive engagement of EULEX in the north of Kosovo.

Such events also act as a reminder of the country's continuing very fragile state of security. Moreover, it is almost impossible to argue that EULEX (and the police sector) has been the only institution playing a crucial role in preventing any new escalation of conflict. Several international organisations, NGOs and foreign embassies are present in Kosovo that pursue their own interests and follow their own agendas, which occasionally run contrary to the general goal of peacebuilding in Kosovo. Hence, one cannot attribute credit for the success in conflict prevention and peacebuilding to just one organisation or mission.

4.1.2 EULEX as a Mediator

In terms of strengthening the police, EULEX has directly and indirectly served as a link between Serbian and Kosovo authorities, in line with the EU's broader engagement in the region: the so-called Serbia–Kosovo dialogue and its "Support to Dialogue Implementation" objective. The EU-facilitated dialogue between Belgrade and Prishtina may be seen as a major example of the EU's positive impact, substantially influencing all areas of the EU's engagement in the region (Interviews 1 2016a and 20 2016r). Some interviewees also argue this shows the EU's potential to foster reconciliation. EULEX's substantive 'middle man' role can, however, be viewed as both positive and negative for Kosovo's long-term development (Interviews 13 2016k and 14 2016l).

On the positive side, EULEX has helped with the normalisation of relations between Kosovo and Serbia by taking steps in the direction of bringing representatives from both sides to the table, establishing the exchange of information, along with a certain degree of coordination and cooperation (Interviews 14 2016l and 15 2016m).[3] The first signs of cooperation between the Kosovar and Serbian border police here were regarded as a successful practice (Interview 15 2016m). This clearly shows that technical cooperation on the tactical level between two countries' police forces, which often have a common goal (e.g. preventing human trafficking), can progress relatively well if not hindered or prevented by 'higher authorities' pursuing their own political agendas, that are often counterproductive for peacebuilding. Further, EULEX has also helped accelerate the integration of former Serbian police staff into the Kosovar Police, and provided basic orientation training courses for officers of Serb ethnicity wishing to join the Kosovo Police (EULEX 2016a).

On the negative side, our interviewees noted that current contacts and exchanges between the Serbian and Kosovo Police are only possible because of EULEX. Without the presence of EULEX, meetings are often cancelled or postponed. When this research was conducted in 2015, several interviewees pointed out that Serbia then preferred to talk only through EULEX, seen then as 'a bridge' between the two countries. An interesting question that arises here is thus what will happen when EULEX eventually ends its mission, and whether the links and cooperation so established will be strong enough to survive the absence of EULEX (Interviews 14 2016l and 19 2016q).

---

[3]Aside from the police sector—peeking into the internal affairs sector more in general—the mission also certified a total of 12,391 copies of original civil and religious registry books of birth, marriage and death, and handed them over to the Ministry of Internal Affairs and the Civil Registration Agency in March 2013. EULEX also assisted Belgrade and Prishtina in establishing six co-located interim crossing points, where both parties share common infrastructure at the same geographical location (Interview 14 2016l; EULEX 2016b).

4.1.3   Cooperation with other Actors

The norms established by the EU as a mediator via its normative power—promoting cooperation—should reflect the EU's own way of acting. The EU should therefore behave according to the norms and standards it promotes. In this field, cooperation between EULEX and KFOR was seen as an example of good practice in civil-military relations (Interview 9 2016h). Cooperation and coordination are established on different levels, such as heads of missions, deputy heads of missions, chiefs of staff, chiefs of security, intelligence, as well as the police.

A joint operation procedure defines the interoperability and comprehensiveness of the mission's goals and operations between EULEX and KFOR. It distinguishes the two missions' procedures and sets the basic framework for them to cooperate. Counterpart representatives of the two missions assessed it as a clear and comprehensive tool that was jointly prepared and coordinated by both missions (Interview 6 2016e). This is quite a new tool that has developed over time when a need for closer coordination was recognised and necessary measures to alleviate the issue were introduced.

Moreover, an actor with normative peacebuilding goals should function as 'a force for good' in a post-conflict society, which in our case means good cooperation and coordination with other prominent actors in this field so as to try to maximise the positive effect. However, a certain lack of coordination was identified in the authority and responsibility over the two institutions in situations where both EULEX police and KFOR military units find themselves in the same field of operation. Some interviewees from KFOR believe the cooperation between EULEX and KFOR is weak due to the widely held opinion among EULEX personnel that KFOR is no longer necessary (e.g. during protests in December 2015 and January 2016 the Kosovo police was in charge of riot control and did very well) (Interview 6 2016e). The quality of cooperation is evaluated somewhat differently and more positively by high-level EULEX officials (Interview 9 2016h). EULEX and KFOR exchange liaison officers on a permanent basis and cooperate in other ways (Interview 20 2016r). Joint trainings have also been introduced to address the issue and increase interoperability in the field.

But while cooperation on riot control between EULEX and KFOR is therefore evaluated as generally good, communication with the Kosovo Police and the consequent coordination of all three responders has occasionally been challenging (Interview 20 2016r). For example, KFOR is the third responder and so must go through EULEX structures if it is to cooperate with the Kosovo police, leading to criticism of the long response times, especially among KFOR staff:

> EULEX should be in the line of communication between the Kosovo and Serbian police. If something happens at the border, the Serbs call EULEX, EULEX calls the Kosovo border police, and the latter calls people on the ground. But for this process they need one day! If there is illegal activity this is useless. The communication does not work /…/ (Interview 17 2016o).

As noted, in extreme cases a whole day may be needed for the communication to proceed and a decision to be taken, which is neither acceptable nor normative in situations requiring an urgent response. EULEX, as the second responder, is especially a link between the Kosovo Police (first responder) and KFOR (third responder). This implies that the quality of communication between KFOR and the Kosovo Police *can only be as good* as the communication between EULEX–KFOR and EULEX–Kosovo Police. Simply put, the relations among the three actors responders (Kosovo Police, EULEX, KFOR) are assessed as somewhat problematic since according to interviews there is a lack of coordination and clear division of responsibilities (Interview 6 2016e).

In terms of the cooperation of the actors engaged in peacebuilding in Kosovo, one must also acknowledge the common trainings hold the potential to boost and enhance the efficiency of the actors while also contributing to overall comprehensiveness. There are positive examples of common trainings, such as the joint EULEX–KFOR training, revealing promising aspects of civil–military cooperation (Interview 20 2016r). Another example of good cooperation occurs between EULEX and the OSCE in the field of training Kosovo Police, where EULEX is continuing the process of police education that started with the Kosovo Police Academy, previously managed by the OSCE (ibid.).

Some of our interviewees believe there are still further possibilities of improvement regarding joint trainings which could flow from joining the resources of several institutions in Kosovo. It would be necessary to strengthen information sharing, for example, in the field of training where EULEX, the OSCE and the International Criminal Investigative Training Assistance Programme (ICITAP) could work together and see what type of training of the Kosovo Police is provided by each organisation (Interviews 1 2016a and 8 2016g). This would not only relieve some of the burden on the EULEX training unit, but also benefit the EULEX budget (Interview 1 2016a).

Finally, the EU can make a positive impact as a normative power in achieving positive ends on the ground through cooperation by visibly correcting the conflict attitudes in this post-conflict society. Regarding specific operational cooperation with local actors,[4] very good coordination is acknowledged relative to the Kosovo Police (especially riot-control units and rapid-reaction forces) and border control. Moreover, EULEX supported the training of the Kosovo Police North Quick Response Team and the integration of 287 Kosovo Serb police officers into the Kosovo Police Command North.

A multi-ethnic specialised unit to protect religious and cultural heritage throughout Kosovo was established with EULEX assistance (EULEX 2016a). The protection of religious and cultural heritage is in line with the values the EU promotes and upholds. Importantly, it is also in line with the goal of achieving outcomes facilitating the building of peace in the country—by protecting the

---

[4]A Joint Rule of Law Coordination Board is the main body for ensuring coordination between EULEX and the locals (Interview 20 2016r).

nation's heritage, or what makes this group distinct, is part of recognising that the opposite side is "a legitimate other" as opposed to a "shameful other" (Lixinski 2013, 108).

In addition, both EULEX and the local Kosovo Police have been cooperating with each other in the police sector and appreciate the effective and timely exchange of information, knowledge-sharing and on-the-ground assistance (Interviews 15 2016m and 19 2016q). However, certain limitations are perceived in relation to the sharing of information. For example, some experts believe the Kosovo Police is occasionally reluctant to share information with EULEX (Interviews 2 2016b and 8 2016g), and *vice versa*, while others think that the cooperation is very efficient (Interview 14 2016l). As seen from the interviews, this perception depends largely on the individual experience and position held by a given EULEX staff member.

The next limit influencing information sharing between the local police and EULEX is technology. Interviewees who work closely with the Kosovo Police noted the lack of certain specialised equipment required for advanced investigations and data-sharing, which may be considered a technical limitation. In order for the Kosovo Police to take full responsibility and ownership over its work, additional efforts should be made to equip and train officers to use this technology.

However, most interviewees agreed the equipment and technologies donated by the international community are seen as a great improvement by local actors since they now have modern technical capabilities to conduct their operations. Border police and customs are generally equipped with very sophisticated technology provided by international donors. A problem that often arises is the lack of continuity and sustainable training for newcomers on how to use such advanced technologies (Interviews 13 2016k and 15 2016m). Therefore, it frequently happens that the modern technology cannot be used properly—or even at all—as newcomers often have no idea how to use it. Despite certain sectors of the police and customs being equipped with adequate technological means, the following shortcomings are noted:

- the lack of appropriate information and communication technology (not all of which meet EU standards); and
- local IT systems are not connected with Europol, Interpol and several other crucial international systems (Interview 14 2016l).

Besides EULEX, considerable donations from the OSCE, ICITAP and individual countries significantly help the Kosovo Police gain both the necessary equipment and knowledge for how to use it (Interview 15 2016m). Several members of the Kosovo Police have also been trained and educated at prestigious police and defence academies in foreign countries (ibid.).

Finally, the relationship between local Kosovo institutions (including the Kosovo Police) and the broader public has been significantly impacted by the infamous EULEX corruption allegations. These has affected the mission's public image among the local population, including its police personnel and its work with the local Kosovo Police. Here we should also note the Jacque Report from April

2015 and the criticism expressed by Capussela (2015), Kursani (2013), Radin (2014) and Malešič and Juvan (2015), as well as the 2012 European Court of Auditors' report (2012).

Such criticism means the loss of trust seen today, reflected in the largely negative perception of EULEX, is no surprise (Qehaja 2017). The situation has been broadly used—and abused—by Kosovar political leaders for their own political gains. This has only further eroded EULEX's credibility among the locals. Yet claims that local leaders are not informed or engaged with the mission, its goals or framework are often politically motivated and do not accurately reflect the true situation (Interview 10 2016i).

4.1.4   European Values, Standards and Practices

The EULEX 2009 programme report states the mission will help move the Kosovo Police's shift towards "adherence to internationally recognised standards and European best practices" (EULEX Programme Report 2009, 7). In this regard, the vast majority of our interviewees noted the Kosovo Police is to be regarded as one of the most successful examples of the EULEX engagement. This can also be attributed to the international community's strategic long-term focus on establishing and developing the capability of the Kosovo Police (Interviews 8 2016g and 11 2016j).

Almost all major international civilian actors in Kosovo (UNMIK, OMIK, and EULEX) claim credit for establishing a functioning Kosovo Police. Statements concerning EULEX's role in training and mentoring Kosovar police must therefore be duly considered in this light and by also considering the earlier work of other international actors. The following EU best practices and concepts are noted as considerably impacting the Kosovo Police's operational capacity (Interviews 2 2016b, 8 2016g, 9 2016h, 15 2016m, 17 2016o and 18 2016p):

- gender, vulnerable groups and minority training;
- community and intelligence-based policing;
- riot-control unit training;
- integrated border management and customs; and
- dealing with sensitive crimes (hate crime, ethnicity-related crime, religion-related crime etc.).

If EULEX is to continue transferring its so-called European practices to the Kosovo Police, due to the rotations of personnel it needs to have a well-established system of pre-deployment training to ensure the efficient transfer of these concepts. Pre-deployment training conducted in several EU member states lacks harmonisation with the police sector and is thus inadequate. Hence, it is not surprising that staff training can vary from very good specialist training to general basic training (Zupančič et al. 2017). This results from uncoordinated training procedures that are mostly left up to the authority and responsibility of the specific contributing state (Interview 8 2016g).

> If we look, for example, at the specific post of border police and customs, we can see that certain participating countries send well-trained border police officers with specialised knowledge and experience, while some (countries) deployed regular police without long-term specialised border knowledge, which results in different levels of knowledge and experience, consequently impacting the quality of EULEX MMA activities (Interview 11 2016j).

When considering the training of EU personnel, the balance of quality and quantity should be taken into account. While the staff believed the sheer amount of training is sufficient, the content and quality of the necessary specialised training is sometimes debatable. Especially when considering important strategic topics, a more tailor-made approach would benefit the overall usefulness and quality of training (Interviews 1 2016a and 4 2016d). An example of such a tailor-made programme is the EU seminars for the Heads of Delegations and the educational training programmes for the Heads of CSDP missions. Nevertheless, these are usually very short-term programmes (usually lasting just one day), so they can hardly be described as specialised or comprehensive staff training (Interview 20 2016r). Some limited joined pre-deployment training is also available for other EULEX staff, usually an introduction and briefing programmes held in Brussels primarily focused on CSDP mission procedures (ibid.).

One positive step here is the establishment of an online database entitled Schoolmaster. The database is to eventually become part of a broader information system called Goalkeeper and contains information on all courses delivered throughout the EU that are relevant to the CSDP. Based on the lessons learned, Goalkeeper has the potential to improve some of the persistent shortcomings of the CSDP training and deployment process (EEAS 2016).

Most interviewees note the great improvement in the training on gender-related topics, a priority across the EU, that is included in the knowledge transferred to the local police. Both international and local staff stated that gender training (in both the pre-deployment phase and on the ground) is showing a positive impact (Interviews 1 2016a, 4 2016d and 6 2016e). In this regard, the EU is upholding its normative values and interests, while also promoting its normative identity as the advocator of the values of gender equality, minority rights, and multi-ethnic society. However, according to some interviews the attitude of local counterparts towards these topics is still occasionally reserved (Interview 6 2016e) and, generally speaking, Kosovo has yet to improve its record in these areas (Haug 2015).

Overall, concerning the use of soft instruments to achieve the 'force for good' status as a normative power in Kosovo, the interviews show that the decision of EULEX to change its initial focus from the judiciary to the police was instrumental for achieving this status. This might be since it is much cheaper and easier to achieve the set goals with the latter, and that the Kosovo Police was not in too poor shape when EULEX took over: "The Kosovo police was found to have a comprehensive legal structure, properly trained and sufficiently skilled staff, an adequate budget, and sufficient equipment to meet its legal objectives" (EULEX 2009, 12).

EULEX officials believe the mission has had a much stronger impact on the police than other sectors (Interview 9 2016h and 15 2016m). EULEX has been relatively successful in providing police training, but the Kosovo Police had already proven it was capable of working without its assistance (especially for low-profile cases not involving white-collar crime or the unlawful activities of political and economic elites). The Police has integrated the border-management aspects of work into its structures and improved its riot control response (Interview 18 2016p).

One could argue that, as a proportion, the money for police (also customs as shown in the following chapters) was relatively well spent compared to the huge sums spent on the judiciary. The overall conclusion of this subchapter is that the Kosovo Police has benefited significantly from EULEX. EULEX has helped the Kosovo Police develop new policing concepts (community-led policing, intelligence-based policing) and related training. Moreover, EULEX has made people more willing to cooperate with the police; police officers are better educated, receive gender and minority training and are more ethnically diverse and more professional in behaviour than before. This may be understood as an attempt to project the existence of 'European values' to a certain country.

EULEX also had an important role in the training of the Kosovo Police in riot control, helping the force to meet the EU's vision of law-enforcement agencies able to operate without international support (EULEX 2009, 7). In addition, the local community generally sees EULEX's intervention in the police sector as no longer necessary because they regard the national capabilities as being sufficient and ready to take over and function independently, especially given the mentioned work of the Kosovo Police (Interviews 13 2016k, 15 2016m and 17 2016o). However, the police still attracts legitimate criticism, such as by Capussela (2015), that it performs poorly in cases of high-profile corruption as well as in cases of white-collar crime and organised crime.

Moreover, EULEX helped facilitate dialogue between Kosovo and Serbia since the first signs of cooperation between the Kosovo Police and its Serbian counterparts may be attributed in part to the role played by EULEX. One might therefore argue the EU has achieved certain normative goals and envisioned outcomes that have added to its identity as a legitimate power in peacebuilding. However, it would be over-ambitious and wrong to declare the EU's identity as a normative power based on analysis of just one actor within its structure.

4.2 The Judiciary

4.2.1 The Judicial System in Kosovo: 1999–2008

Following the end of NATO's military operation in June 1999 and the withdrawal of FRY institutions from Kosovo, the international actors tasked with peace- and state-building faced a shortfall of educated and trained experts able to effectively administer justice in Kosovo. Namely, most administrative positions in Kosovo prior to 1999 were held by Serbs for two reasons: firstly, at the time, they were treated preferentially and, secondly, the Albanians had started boycotting Serb-dominated institutions upon the rise of nationalism and the measures introduced at the expense of Kosovo Albanians (Yannis 2004; Weller 2009).

The can be illustrated by considering some numbers. For example, in 1999 just 30 out of the 756 judges and prosecutors in Kosovo were Kosovo Albanians, with the Kosovo Albanian majority even seeing them as collaborators with Milošević's regime or traitors (Skendaj 2014a, 88). These figures changed dramatically after June 1999 when NATO's military campaign brought about an end to Serbian rule over Kosovo. After the summer of 1999, only a handful of experts of Serbian nationality (police officers, prosecutors and judges) remained in Kosovo. They generally refused to participate in the newly emerging justice system being set up by UNMIK. Those who had left for Serbia with the retreating armed forces took with them official property and court documents (Zupančič 2015).

After the 1999 ceasefire, the OSCE—as one of the four main international organisations responsible for post-conflict reconstruction—considered bringing in international jurists to Kosovo to fill the previously described vacuum. But UNMIK as an umbrella organisation did not agree to bringing the 'internationals' into a war-torn society. The OSCE plan was different: trying to identify Kosovo Albanian judges and prosecutors in refugee camps and bring them back to Kosovo, where they would work together with the international judges brought to the war-torn country. UNMIK rejected the proposal out of "concern that adding international judges and prosecutors to their executive and legislative power would make them vulnerable to accusations of neo-colonialism" (Skendaj 2014a, 89).

Moreover, many UN officials believed that Kosovo was able to handle its own administration. Finally, at the time international jurists were not included on the 'institutional development checklist'; including international judges and prosecutors in national judicial systems was unprecedented before the creation of hybrid courts in Kosovo. Therefore, at first UNMIK only took the liberty of appointing local judges and prosecutors to the so-called Emergency Judicial System. Interestingly, not a single Kosovo Serb was appointed, which reflected substantial bias against Kosovo Serbs and other ethnic minorities in Kosovo (ibid.).[5] On the other hand, it

---

[5]Skendaj (2014a, 89–90) mentions the problem of the prolonged detaining of accused Kosovo Roma or Serbs even on insubstantial charges, while the KLA members would be released and cleared of charges immediately. He writes that "the Kosovo Albanian judges and prosecutors were under tremendous political and social pressure to favour their ethnic kin. The jurists could lose their jobs, be denied promotion, or face threats against their lives. Politicians could threaten the judges and prosecutors in order to stop the prosecutions of people connected to them. /…/ After ten years of systematic repression against Kosovo Albanians, the neighbours and contacts also exercised pressure on the Kosovo judges and prosecutors to be harsh on the Kosovo Serbs and Roma and easy on the Kosovo Albanian 'war heroes'. Human rights activists regarded such detentions as violating the rights of the detainees and the activity that undermines the judicial independence of the local courts. Also, KFOR at the time used similar detention procedures—if KFOR believed that a person could pose a danger to stability, he or she would be detained in KFOR facility for a time period to be determined by KFOR itself (ibid.).

has to be noted that the ambitions of Kosovo Serbs at the time to join the institutions of the newly-emerging country were extremely low. These characteristics of the judicial system were indeed problematic, especially given the international actors wanted the local judges to focus on interethnic and political crimes, namely, two types that are particularly difficult to address in post-conflict societies.

In order to address the bias against the Serbs and other ethnic minorities among Kosovo Albanian judges, UNMIK finally introduced a programme of international judges and prosecutors, reaching this decision incrementally over time. This radical shift came because Kosovo's sovereignty rested with UNMIK—the international judges and prosecutors could take on cases involving any type of crime, including those already assigned to local judges (Skendaj 2014a, 89–91).

The judicial system therefore formally fell within UNMIK's authority because the system was essentially related to security; in other words, the international actors were worried about the possible flaring up of inter-ethnic tensions, or any attempts in meddling and intimidation in the judicial system that might endanger the rule of law. Put differently, the concern of the international actors in Kosovo was that "crimes against ethnic minorities and crimes committed by political elites would not be prosecuted" (ibid.). Moreover, the economic stagnation of Kosovo that had created poverty and unemployment during UNMIK's rule was identified as likely to expose the country to the risk of social unrest and political instability (Capussela 2015, 42).

The UNMIK mandate included the creation of an independent, impartial and multi-ethnic judiciary with high standards of competence and professional ability (Report of the Secretary-General, 1999). UNMIK held legislative and executive powers, including administration of the judiciary. These powers were exercised by UNMIK's chief administrator, the head of the mission, and the SRSG (Cerone and Baldwin 2003, 28). His role as the sole legislator and executive authority holding the power to administer and appoint officials to the judiciary showed the centralisation of power with the goal of coordinating the international administration (Skendaj 2014a, 88).

Kosovar courts under UNMIK are counted among 'hybrid' or 'internationalised' courts (Cerone and Baldwin 2003, 26). The system derived its competence from UNMIK mission regulations and was composed of both national and international judges and prosecutors trained in applying laws of both a national and international character. However, the system was unique by virtue, as it did not have a fixed internationalised court or panel. Rather, the judges were sitting on the panels in Kosovo on a case-by-case basis. Further, the courts' competence overlapped with the International Criminal Tribunal for the former Yugoslavia (ibid.).

However, UNMIK's administration over the judicial sector proved problematic. Skendaj (2014a, 91) notes that the "inclusion of international judges and prosecutors did not insulate the local jurists from political and social pressure". UNMIK appointed judges based on recommendations of the Transitional Council composed, paradoxically, of local political leaders. Moreover, the newly established Advisory Judicial Commission failed to discipline certain judges and prosecutors despite evidence of misconduct.

Recruitment procedures in the judiciary were also inadequate. Almost no new judges were recruited between 2001 and 2008; the measures to reduce backlogs were not taken; merit was not a factor in either recruitment or promotion since Kosovar judges had no system for evaluating their performance in place. No security measures were taken to protect the judges and their families when dealing with difficult political crimes, making them easily vulnerable to incentives offered by political elites. The training of judges was also not systematic, whereas the internationals were often unfamiliar with the legal framework of Kosovo (Skendaj 2014a, 91–92).

UNMIK's administration of the judiciary did not bring the expected results as it did not manage to build up capacity in this sector. Skendaj (2014a, 96) even states that "when multiple donors funded various consultants to work on the same policy without coordination, technical assistance was wasted because the local bureaucracy did not gain knowledge and capacity. When the international donors have been divided, local politicians have played them against each other".

4.2.2 EULEX's Arrival and the Kosovo Judiciary

It soon became clear that the root causes of the dysfunctional rule-of-law system in the country should be re-examined with high priority after Kosovo's proclamation of independence. Judicial reform, if successful, would also affect the performance of economic institutions (Zupančič et al. 2017, 5).[6] To achieve this, the EU struck upon an idea: to launch a CSDP mission to improve the rule of law in Kosovo.

Capussela (2015, 114) notes that "EULEX was asked to improve the rule of law precisely in order to allow the economy to grow and stabilize the country: and a crucial precondition for doing so was reducing impunity for corruption and organized crime, which Kosovo's institutions and endogenous forces were unwilling or unable to do". EULEX was therefore deployed immediately after the country's independence, thereby placing the judiciary in the EU's hands. This overtaking of the judiciary by the EU is, more than in any other sector, a clear reflection of the EU's efforts to be seen as a normative actor. The overarching aim within the mandate concerning the judiciary was for the branch to become "sustainably accountable, independent, multi-ethnic and free from political interference" (Capussela 2015, 107). As mentioned, EULEX was tasked with two different sets of responsibilities: first, to monitor, mentor and advise (from 2012 on, Strengthening Division) and, second, to directly exercise judicial powers (Executive Division).

---

[6]One of the main pillars of the *ordoliberal* peacebuilding lies in "building a strong state through the construction of a social-moral order, which is why rule of law must be upheld" (Zupančič et al. 2017, 5). A functional state can create the institutional environment for the normal functioning of a liberal economy. *Ordoliberal* theory does not identify itself with a weak state at the mercy of economic forces, but a strong state that restrains competition and secures the social and ideological preconditions of economic liberty (Bonefeld 2012 in Zupančič et al. 2017).

4.2.3   General Normative Misconception of the Executive Mandate for the Judiciary

The strengthening part of EULEX's *mandate* is in line with the EU's normative character; it presents itself as a force for good, aiming to improve the functioning of the institutions that are a precondition for the development and democratisation of the country. Moreover, it focuses on the empowerment of society (normative interest) and is in line with the EU values of democracy, rule of law, local ownership and multi-ethnic institutions. If performed well, it can possibly have a correcting influence.

However, the EULEX Executive Division is focused on delivering rule-of-law services until the local authorities become professional enough and the executive functions can be fully transferred to them (EULEX 2016c). Already this part of the mandate completely dismantles the EU's interest to empower society—since, in fact, it takes away its sovereign right (that the EU helped it obtain) to have control over its own criminal justice, over its citizens and its territory. This is a non-normative behaviour of an EU institution, making the assertion that Kosovo is a protectorate seem legitimate (Capussela 2015). On the other hand, it is difficult to argue from the perspective of a functioning rule-of-law sector that local judges and prosecutors should take over all the responsibilities from the very beginning, without being properly trained to perform the work.

While the local community commonly perceives EULEX and its executive engagement as no longer necessary in the fields of customs and the police (Interview 13 2016k, 15 2016m and 17 2016o; Qehaja 2017), only a handful of people identify the Kosovar judiciary as capable and efficient (Interview 15 2016m). However, several EU member states argue that EULEX is doing all the work as local institutions are perceived as incapable, thus inflating their responsibility towards the other extreme. Again, every two years, when the need to extend EULEX's mandate is in question, we can see a clear motivation to extend the mission's mandate by another two years also among EU officials; namely, EULEX is by far the largest CSDP mission and thus offers a considerable number of well-paid jobs that would be threatened by the mission's sudden closure (Grilj and Zupančič 2016).

All of these findings can be seen as reflecting a self-empowering interest, not based on genuine peacebuilding normative values of doing good, and especially not in line with the declared normative behaviour. It should be noted that local structures often try to portray themselves as more effective than they perhaps really are, and thus see a foreign agency as a threat to their public credibility (Interview 15 2016m). This leads to the mission encountering local contestation from several angles (Qehaja 2017; Mahr 2017) and the normative goal of establishing attitudes in the society that would lead to a brighter future cannot be perceived as achieved in this case.

Moreover, the EU claims it wants to create an independent and transparent judicial system, but acted differently when planning EULEX's mandate. This regards the status and organisational allocation of judges in the mission, which definitely creates a legal dilemma: the norm of independence of the judiciary may be questioned due to the mission's structure and the constitutional meaning of the separation of powers is not being respected as the police, prosecutors and judges are all part of the same organisational division (Interview 3 2016c). While judges and prosecutors are, structurally speaking, separated within different departments, the true separation is not really possible as they are still part of the same division and leadership structure, led by the same division head (Interview 16 2016n). Several interviewees described this structure of the mission as a bad practice.

4.2.4 Normativity and the Transfer of European Values

Besides its role in security and the judiciary, the EU has a fundamental transformative role that affects all levels of Kosovo society. 'EU values and standards' make up the core of the reforms EULEX is trying to enforce and this lie in the centre of its normative functioning. Therefore, when assessing the EU's supposed normative character, it is important to also take into account the EU's own values, procedures and code of conduct.

As some interviewees noted, staff from non-EU states often have limited knowledge of EU values and procedures. The problem usually arises when non-EU countries contribute staff to higher (strategic) levels of the mission. Such workers might not be the most appropriate for these positions from the perspective of the EU's values, procedures and best practices, because they come from a different environment (outside the EU). For example, staff members from the USA, Turkey and certain other states were, mentioned when discussing the lack of understanding of EU values, procedures and code of conduct (Interviews 6 2016e and 8 2016g; Zupančič et al., 2017).

This is also a problem with staff, which is *seconded* from EU countries. The main recruitment instrument in CSDP missions generally is secondment (experts sent to the mission by a certain country, which also pays them salary and provides for other benefits related to deployment), while *contracting* (a contract-based relationship between an expert and the mission itself) is used secondarily, mostly to fill gaps not filled with seconded staff before (Interview 20 2016r). On top of this, the lack of standardised selection procedures at the national level is persistently seen as a challenge (Interview 11 2016j). Due to the non-standardised procedures the quality and qualifications of the seconded staff who are selected can vary significantly (Interviews 1 2016a and 10 2016i). The outcomes of these challenging recruitment and selection processes may thus affect broader capabilities and the mission's efficiency (Interview 8 2016g; Grilj and Zupančič 2016).

Instances of EU member states sending workers with inadequate language and cultural skills are also identified as a problem, like with staff from non-EU countries (Interviews 1 2016a, 10 2016i and 11 2016j). Part of the responsibility lies with the member states and another part can be attributed to the interview panel at the mission level, which has a final say in recruiting candidates (Interview 10 2016i). Last but not least, the human resources department must also ensure that important

EULEX posts are dispersed relatively evenly among the EU member states. In other words, the likelihood of being recruited as a EULEX judge, for instance, also depends on a candidate's country of origin and whether that country is already under- or over-represented in EULEX.

Moreover, the different backgrounds of incoming staff create a challenge for the mission of how to ensure continuity in its MMA engagements, while having internal differences in perceptions and understandings of common EU practices (or a lack of them). Most interviewees agreed this is a fundamental issue in the field of operational capability that needs to be addressed (Interviews 1 2016a, 2 2016b and 11 2016j). A challenge in shaping a common approach was noted especially among EULEX judges because they also come from very diverse judicial backgrounds and traditions, with different experience (for example, judges from the United Kingdom with a common law background and the judges from the majority of EU states that have a civil law tradition).

> Being a judge in Greece is unlike being a judge in the United Kingdom, which has a different judicial system, but both judges are expected to apply the same laws once they begin working in EULEX. Nation-specific skill sets and backgrounds must thus be taken into consideration when evaluating the skills and background of personnel (Interview 1 2016a).

While diversity and exposure to a range of backgrounds and traditions is generally a sought-after quality among the judges, a certain level of standardisation and pre-deployment training would also benefit the judiciary (Interview 16 2016n).

This is not only important when discussing the EU's normative behaviour, but is clearly problematic also because the EU is unable to train its 'own' personnel to uphold the values it wants to transfer to Kosovo. Namely, judges seconded to EULEX will, after their secondments expire, most likely return to work in the country that seconded them. This will, at best, take place in a few years' time; often the seconded judges return back home relatively soon. Thus, it remains a challenge to make a judge consider him- or herself as an 'EU judge' only while deployed on a CSDP mission.

These inadequacies are also a problem from the point of view of the normative ends; if the EU with its peacebuilding character wishes to leave a long-lasting footprint in Kosovo by transforming it into a peaceful society, it should be engaging in the efficient cultivation of corrective attitudes and improve the identified inefficiencies instead of ignoring—or even deliberately not addressing—them for the sake of stability, as noted by Capussela (2015).

Both international and local employees warn about the negative implications of the relatively short-duration deployments of EULEX staff. This directly affects this CSDP mission's operational capacities and efficiency. While staff contracted directly by Brussels/the mission usually stay in Kosovo for several years, staff seconded by member states are often deployed for relatively short periods, usually a year or less, with limited opportunity for contract renewal (Cierco and Reis 2014, 654; Grilj and Zupančič 2016).

Due to the relatively short deployments, there is not enough time for newcomers to "catch up with the speed" of the mission and, when they finally do, their turn is already over (Interview 16 2016n). If someone is thus deployed for one year, their effective deployment (including annual leave, sick leave and training) will only be about 6–7 months. This is especially disturbing when assessing continuity on the strategic level (leadership), where long-term commitments are a must. As noted by some interviewees, a strategic-level employee needs at least one year to "get into" the system and become well acquainted with it and to acquire the necessary knowledge on local Kosovar issues in order to operate effectively. It also takes time to establish a relationship of trust with local counterparts in order to be able to conduct, for example, effective bilateral meetings and negotiations (Interviews 7 2016f and 8 2016g).

> One of the complaints that Kosovo people will tell (is that) 12 months is pretty short. And each new employee is working in his own way, even though they have similar viewpoints. If I could, I would keep the team for longer than 1 year. Some countries allow this—Italians for 3 years, French 5 years … people need to learn how to operate, what the local habits are, how things work etc. (Interview 1 2016a).

These short-term jobs are also more attractive to younger and (often) less experienced professionals (Jacque 2015). Of special concern is an issue that occurs with judiciary staff as member states are unwilling to provide their *best* judges and prosecutors since they are needed at home (Zupančič et al. 2017). Moreover, differences in pay among employees from various states working in similar positions, due to the different secondment policies, affect employees' motivation (Interviews 9 2016h and 10 2016i). This is particularly important for the motivation of highly specialised staff, for example of judges and prosecutors. CSDP missions find it difficult to provide financial motivation to expert staff that is stimulating enough for them to leave their well-paid and secure jobs at home and come to Kosovo to work for EULEX.

The mission has been trying to solve or at least mitigate this issue by seconding 'cheaper' judges and prosecutors from certain economically less developed EU countries where the pay received by deployed staff is (compared to their pay back home) much higher but still below that in western EU countries. While this does not automatically imply these judges are in any way less qualified for the job, it does reveal an important challenge of the mission. This research has pointed out certain weaknesses in staff selection, yet the mission's internal evaluation system generally paints a different picture, showing that the majority of staff are performing very well or above expectations (Interview 20 2016r). The relatively big difference between the internal system and the interviews conducted anonymously may indicate shortcomings in the mission's internal review mechanism.

Last but not least, we concur with Cierco and Reis (2014) who argue that the high staff turnover rates cause legal and operational inconsistencies. Based on these findings, we may claim the EU's effort is insufficient for achieving long-lasting change, especially since the problem has already been identified during EULEX's lifetime and reported to Brussels on several occasions (Interviews 15 2016m and 16 2016n).

Nevertheless, local contracted staff were identified as very helpful in this respect as they are usually contracted for longer periods, meaning they have both organisational and cultural knowledge, as well as the requisite contacts. The assistance they give the international staff is thus important for the mission's long-term continuity and sustainability (Interviews 2 2016b and 8 2016g). Enhanced pre-deployment training, education on history, culture and other aspects related to cultural awareness could accelerate the adaptation time needed and improve the newcomers' efficiency (Interview 3 2016c).

4.2.5   The Success and Challenges of EULEX Judges and Prosecutors in the Local Context

Although we have already touched on the work motivation aspect of the EU's judicial personnel that might influence perceptions of the EU as a genuine peace-building actor, we must also consider whether the EU is perceived as a true force for good by the locals.

Work motivation varies between contracted and seconded staff; however, it would be incorrect to make any hasty generalisations. The interviewees noted the locally contracted staff are mostly motivated by excellent salaries, especially compared to the low local salaries (EULEX local staff are usually paid several times more than employees at Kosovo institutions holding similar positions). Due to relatively high salaries received by this small circle of 'chosen locals' at the mission, the local environment often regards them as a privileged elite. In the last few years when EULEX has been reducing staff, this may also have exerted a limited impact on the support for EULEX in the local community as a certain number of people were about to lose their well-paid jobs (Interview 6 2016e). From a methodological viewpoint, it has to be noted that, generally speaking, local staff working for EULEX was not willing to share any critical opinions about EULEX with the researchers.

What does that indicate with regard to the normativity of the EU's means, goals and outputs? Clearly it is not the EU's altruistic character pushing the locals to work for the EU, therefore the EU is not fully capable of attracting the public in a post-conflict society only through normative means, but economic ones as well—something to be expected in poor, war-torn societies. Yet, in terms of the outcome of using such economic means compared to normative means, we can talk of a deepening division in society ('chosen locals') and a paradox commonly known as dependency syndrome. Kosovar society may become, and in the opinion of many (Capussela 2015; Cigler 2017) already is, 'addicted' to the international aid and the continuing presence of the EULEX mission since it brings employment and stimulates the local economy. In this sense, the normative ends are not being achieved.

When assessing the judicial aspects of EULEX's normative influence, the locals' second point was that EULEX is generally perceived as spending too much time examining alleged war crimes and not paying enough attention to organised crime and corruption (Interview 19 2016q). This could in part be attributed to the over-ambitious expectations initially set by the mission's leaders and the highest political figures of the EU, such as Javier Solana, then EUHR for the CSFP:

> The mission will be crucial for the consolidation of rule of law in Kosovo, and furthermore, the development of rule of law and strengthening of multi-ethnic institutions will be to the benefit of all communities in Kosovo. The mission is proof of the EU's strong commitment towards the Western Balkans and it will contribute to the enhancement of stability in the whole region (Council of the European Union 2008b).

Another reason is the poorly communicated essence of the rule-of-law concept that is consistent with the public's general dissatisfaction with EULEX's role in the judiciary and the rule-of-law reform process (Interview 18 2016p). The EU's wider role in Kosovo is complex, having gradually developed from its initial function as the fourth pillar of UNMIK—dealing primarily with economic reconstruction and development—to today's much broader engagement (Zupančič et al. 2017).

The EU is nowadays present in Kosovo chiefly through the EUSR and the European Union office in Kosovo (2017). Parallel to this, EULEX is dealing with the rule of law. The complexity of this engagement is difficult to communicate to the local public (Interview 20 2016r). Combined with the poor public image, this explains why the mission has never really been perceived as part of local society and not constituted an integral part of local life (Interview 19 2016q). On the other hand, as Mahr (2017) notes, the EU as an institution remains a relatively well-trusted actor in Kosovo.

Despite this, the mission is often still perceived as foreign, perhaps even imposed on the local environment. Certain political parties, most notably Vetëvendosje (Self-Determination), build their programmes and political actions on insisting that EULEX and other international organizations should withdraw from Kosovo, as international actors only prolong the dependence of Kosovo and block its independent development. Thus, local actors have often been reluctant to cooperate, or worse, worked hard to make it impossible for EULEX to prosecute someone from their ranks.[7] The latter is a main reason for the local contestation seen among Kosovo Albanians (Mahr 2017).

Second, local judges, prosecutors and politicians have often been 'hiding behind EULEX' and pointing the finger at international actors to deflect attention from their own inefficiency, mismanagement or lack of capacity. The excuse 'this is a task for EULEX' is commonly heard and a prime example of the limits of local ownership. Such a combination of internal protectionism and excuses of local actors

---

[7]Capussela (2015, 117) in his Annex to the book Statebuilding in Kosovo analyses the cases of Fatmir Limaj (an effective military commander) and Hashim Thaçi (the current president), where EULEX failed to achieve satisfactory results "not only because fighting serious crime is a complex enterprise, as the mission and many analysts correctly remark, but also because it disregarded its mandate". In some cases regarding these two high-ranking leaders, EULEX conducted "no investigations, or issued no indictments, despite the fact that it disposed of credible and well-documented evidence strongly suggesting that serious crimes had been committed". On the other hand, local elites rejecting the authority of EULEX when it comes to prosecuting their own. Skendaj (2014a, 73) writes that "when EULEX investigated offices and houses of the minister of transport, Fatmir Limaj, in May 2010, the prime minister claimed that such independent investigations were a violation of Kosovo's institutions. However, according to the constitution and the Ahtisaari plan, EULEX had the authority to investigate such crimes".

has impacted the chances of improving local ownership and the overall efficiency of EULEX's efforts (Interview 19 2016q).

Local institutions' general ability to take over responsibility from EULEX varies from sector to sector, task to task. After years of a prominent international presence, especially in a country established with considerable international assistance, the transfer of tasks to local institutions is challenging. A key lesson is that influential locals can play a significant role in post-conflict reform.

Removing influential local leaders from key positions would most likely destabilise the country and undermine the process (Interview 20 2016r). EULEX staff are well aware that quite a few prominent leaders (like members of the KLA with enormous social and now also economic capital, often regarded as heroes) who would have no difficulty mobilising the electorate to go onto the streets of Kosovo and demonstrate against 'the internationals', bringing the possibility of violence in the blink of an eye. Yet, the price of stability, namely the reluctance to prosecute certain key individuals, is an often criticised element of EULEX's work (and the EU's engagement in general) and thus seen as a failure in preventing political interference and tackling high-level crime.

At the start of this subchapter, we considered a recent case illustrating such a state of affairs. It is necessary for the EU to realise that sacrificing its legitimacy for political stability might also impact the legitimacy of its overall peacebuilding endeavours. In this sense, in the judicial sector at least, it is evident that the 'normative power Europe' is difficult to realise. It is clear that when it comes to the politically-heavy involvement that the EU is disregarding its own mission's goals and principles, its own values of local ownership and fighting corruption, while also failing to meet the desired outcomes since corruption continues in modern Kosovo (European Commission 2012; Transparency International 2016).

Hence, EULEX needs to make the local community understand that law exists above the unwritten local rules: no easy task (Interview 20 2016r). The interviews in general reveal the rule of law has not been fully implemented in Kosovo given that there are still too many local networks with the power to discourage the locals from speaking out against them, despite the existence of evidence (Interviews 6 2016e, 15 2016m and 18 2016p).

> If you want to prosecute a politician, of course they will run a campaign against you— hence EULEX is not popular (Interview 17 2016o).

One problem which remains is that EULEX officials too often give locals what they have, but not what they need. To be able to give people what they need, you need to know the situation, culture, tradition etc. (Interviews 1 2016a and 17 2016o). Thus, EULEX has never become an integral part of Kosovar society (Qehaja 2017; Interview 19 2016q). One case of interest is that Kosovars are more interested in the pursuit of crimes happening *since* the war (e.g. corruption, crime) than war crimes, yet EULEX is still mainly focused on the latter (Interviews 9 2016h and 18 2016p).

A paradoxical example of post-war corruption is the international assistance provided. Among the other international actors, the investment, donations and assistance money provided by the USA have to be considered first given that it is one of the biggest stakeholders in the country next to the EU. One would therefore expect a high level of coordination to exist between the EU and US investment, donation and assistance efforts yet, as stated by some interviewees, that is often not the case. This leads to duplication, unnecessary investments in the same or similar projects and ultimately a waste of money. The project on the civil code is an example that is mentioned.

> There's a USD 8 million project run by the Americans, and a EUR 4 million project by the EU on the same topic. In addition, there's money spent by the OSCE. Some local actors are abusing such duplication for their own personal gains (Interview 10 2016i).

Local stakeholders are understandably interested in receiving money from various sources, even if the purpose of using the funds is often dubious. In order to prevent such misuse, a better overview and greater coordination are required— however much a cliché this might sound (ibid.). Such a waste of EU funds and the locals' perceptions of the EU's efforts in the framework of a post-conflict society do not speak well for the EU's role as a normative peacebuilding actor. This again shows while the EU might be relatively successful in fulfilling its technical role, its political role and the legitimacy of its aims often come into question due to absence of strong internal political agreement among the EU member states on what Kosovar society should look like in the future.

Last but not least, one has to be quite careful to avoid making too hasty conclusions about the supposed ineffectiveness of EULEX's judiciary, sometimes exclusively wrongly ascribed to the incapability of EULEX itself. Namely, in the geopolitical context where international actors have such divergent and often contrary agendas, it is difficult to blame a single agency for all failures, let alone the fact that not even the EU member states are unanimous on Kosovo's political future as an independent state.

4.2.6   Future Challenges for Kosovo's Judiciary

One of the current challenges facing the Kosovar judiciary is integrating Serb judges and administrative staff into it. Namely, the judges and prosecutors in the north of Kosovo, who are mainly Serbs, refused to become part of the Kosovar justice system after the FRY *de facto* lost control over Kosovo in 1999.[8] The wish to integrate Kosovo Serb judges into Kosovo's judicial institutions is due to the

---

[8]As mentioned, after the end of war in Kosovo, the judges and prosecutors in the north of Kosovo operated as part of the FRY (later Serbia and Montenegro; later the Republic of Serbia) judicial system, only answering to the authorities in Belgrade. Later on, the authority of UNMIK was recognised, and thus the justice system in the north of Kosovo started to operate as a conglomerate of UNMIK and FRY/Serbian laws. However, after 2008 this was replaced by local laws, with exception of those courts in the north of Kosovo which continued to use SFRY's laws, declaring themselves part of the Serbian justice system which also pays their wages.

broader-than-EULEX *political* dialogue between Kosovo and Serbia led by the EU, in an attempt to persuade local powerholders to secure some sort of stability in Kosovo. In February 2015, an agreement to integrate Serbian judges and prosecutors into Kosovo's judiciary for work in northern Kosovo municipalities was reached (Aliu 2017).

However, the EU's involvement in the negotiations is inconsistent with EULEX's objective to develop this multi-ethnic judiciary transparently and "free from political interference", as the appointment of judges was a result of political actions whose meaning may be called into question by both Albanian and Serbian political elites, according to one former employee of EULEX, Andrea Capussela (2015). This has been a source of the locals' contestation against EULEX that constituted a very important element of the revolt of Kosovar society (Mahr 2017).

In his book, Capussela (2015) states that the Serb and Kosovar elites have shared certain interests ever since when it comes to cooperating with the international community. However, Capussela warns against the political exploitation in this regard: "Yet such leaders benefit from the support of the international community— which their party 'owes existence' to—because they serve as a visible symbol of Kosovo's 'multi-ethnic' character" (Capussela 2015, 88–89).

Therefore, on one hand the EU may be considered as a positive peacebuilding actor since occasions like the integration of Serbian judges into Kosovo's judiciary suggest a real improvement in the otherwise tense political situation in Kosovo. The EU, aspiring to be a successful peacebuilder, also emphasises the need for local ownership in reform of the judiciary, which presumes 'broad and inclusive negotiations and compromise building'. As such, the reform is supposedly aimed at others-empowerment. However, the EU's approach to local ownership is often based on quite a technocratic approach often lacking in efficient communication channels that could be effectively used by all local actors (Mac Ginty 2017; Ejdus and Juncos 2017). Further, with its allegedly normative behaviour the EU weakens the role of its own EULEX mission in the field. EULEX is tasked with facilitating the creation of an independent and multi-ethnic judiciary, but by seeking consensus it again places power into the hands of local elites.

Expressed differently, is the EU really correcting the attitudes of this post-conflict society or merely casting shadows in 'Plato's cave', able to deceive the eyes of the international community? The EU facilitated the dialogue that led to the establishment of a more multi-ethnic judiciary based on the European insistence on local ownership whereby it left decisions in the negotiations up to local leaders. This can be seen as a genuine normative end given the final outcome was indeed the establishment of multi-ethnic courts. However, Ejdus (2017) comments that the concept of local ownership in this case is focused on the local powerholders or elites that directly benefit from EULEX's policies. In this way, it simply helps further consolidate their grips on power. This could be interpreted as the EU sacrificing its long-term legitimacy and sustainability for the sake of short-term stability.

In the words of the representative of one local NGO:

How is the EU going to send a mission to fight the criminals who have unintentionally but willingly transformed into the EU's best partners for stability? Even if the EU sent an army of prosecutors, judges and police, it would fail because the EU is not ready to 'risk' a little and say perhaps that if they fight these criminals they will not sacrifice stability after all. The EU did not and does not want to 'gamble' even a little on this. So it is a matter of geopolitics, internal parameters within the EU, it is the idea of success on paper etc. that is preventing any real success.

To sum up, we can criticise the power the EU places in the hands of leaders who 'behave well' (both current presidents of Serbia and Kosovo) that could be misused for their own purposes; for example, it is said Kosovo President Hashim Thaçi could be prosecuted in up to eight cases (mainly concerning corruption and organised crime) (Capussela 2015, 117–119).

Yet, at the same time, this book can complement the EU's ability to help make a step forward in the integration of these two post-conflict communities, for decades separated and torn apart by war. On 6 November 2017 judges of Serbian nationality —despite strong contestation in early stages—started working within Kosovo's judiciary, thereby completing the task of integration in that area. In 2017, 13 prosecutors and 33 administrative staff from non-majority communities were integrated in northern Kosovo, while 41 judges and 107 civil servants were appointed across the Kosovar judiciary (Kosovo Prosecutorial Council 2017). This surely heralds more productive relations between Kosovo Albanians and Kosovo Serbs in the future.

Putting aside the challenge of integrating Serbian judges and prosecutors and now turning to the mission's outcomes, the official figures on EULEX's executive tasks show the mission has been involved in several cases. Since the beginning of the EULEX mission, Kosovo's Special Prosecution Office has been involved in different stages of proceedings in approximately 1350 cases, with currently more than 100 cases still in progress. EULEX has also been involved in over 42,700 conflict-related property cases through the Kosovo Property Claims Commission (EULEX 2016a). Many of these were inter-ethnic in character (Interview 20 2016r).

Nevertheless, Capussela (2015) states the actual results of EULEX's work in the judiciary in Kosovo are poor. "Considering how widespread political corruption and organized crime are in Kosovo, these results are gravely inadequate: averages of 2.5 indictments and 0.7 convictions per year, and 0.3 convictions per indictment, can neither repress nor deter such phenomena. Assuming that those involved in serious crime /.../ are as few as 1600 (ten times the number of SHIK's salaried members in 2003, or one sixth of the KLA's strength and 0.09% of the population), over the past six years each of them faced a cumulative of 0.25% risk of being convicted" (Capussela 2015, 118). He candidly adds that "despite EULEX's deployment, therefore, serious crime was an effectively risk-free profession" (ibid.).

Moreover, when Capussela (2015) looked deeper into the cases of the 'leading figures' of Kosovo, such as those involving Fatmir Limaj and Hashim Thaçi, he discovered that on some occasions EULEX conducted no investigation or issued no indictment despite holding evidence strongly indicating serious crimes had been committed. Some cases were in fact opened only after EULEX became aware its inaction would soon be discovered, after its inaction had already been discovered, or after EU or international public opinion demanded an investigation. In certain cases, EULEX convicted secondary figures and did not investigate higher ranking ones. In two cases inspected out of 23, EULEX only appealed the one where the elites had a smaller interest.

Capussela (2015, 121) also suggests that in at least 15 out of 23 inspected cases concerning two members of the elite, EULEX arranged for investigations by the police, prosecutors and judges that strongly suggest "the mission tended not to prosecute high-level crime, and, when it had to, it sought not to indict or convict prominent figures". Revelations like this cast a dark shadow over EULEX's normative character as well as the 'normative power EU' argument.

This raises an important question: how did this all happen? Why was the mission left to perform so poorly in some aspects? Capussela states (2015, 224–225) the mission is failing (in his view, completely) due to the insufficient incentives provided by management to work according to the EU's interests, while the EU was unable to move out of the area: the Kosovo crisis on the occasion the CSDP was practically born, and EULEX is the EU's flagship mission. Moreover, according to Capussela the sums of money invested in Kosovo are basically unprecedented: the overall cost for the EU and the member states exceeds EUR 1 billion.

With the goal of shedding light on EULEX's normative power character, we may conclude the EU and its personnel hold the potential to contribute to peace, yet the mission's planning and actual capabilities often prevent it from acting effectively. In the words of one interviewee: "I know cases where three or four different judges have worked on one case (they had to leave after 6 months)" (Interview 19 2016q). Further, the mission's success often depends on the motivations and effectiveness of a person holding a certain position. However, the biggest problem is that this mission does not reflect others-empowering interests, but often uses the local elites as a factor to ensure stability, even though they might have an ulterior purpose for becoming involved.

First, stability in Kosovo means stability in the Balkans—the EU's backyard. Second, stability in Kosovo allows the EULEX flagship mission to be perceived as relatively successful in the international community's eyes—creating a (shallow) image of the EU as a new normative player in the world. But the normative outcomes presented above in the case of the judiciary have not 'corrected' the problematic behaviour in Kosovo—the 'big fish' are still free to swim around the world of politics—meaning the possible threat of violent conflict continues to exist.

4.3   Customs

After the war in Kosovo ended in 1999 and following the withdrawal of the FRY's institutions, one of the first bodies to be created to help fill the security and political vacuum in Kosovo was the customs service. It officially began operating on 3

September 1999. It was established as a Customs Service within the UNMIK pillar aimed at ensuring the fair and consistent application of customs rules and other provisions (Skendaj 2014a).

As the "final state bureaucracy" (Skendaj 2014b, 466), the role of the customs service is to "collect revenue for the state budget and facilitate the movement of goods and people across borders" (ibid.). The service is responsible for collecting general revenue at the international borders and therefore provides important state budget revenues. As mentioned in previous chapters, the international actors in Kosovo believed in the idea of a market economy with a fiscally responsible state and strong government able to manage its own budget in a democratic, transparent and responsible way.

4.3.1 Establishing a New Customs Service (1999–2008)

When preparations for the post-conflict reconstruction of Kosovo were starting in 1999, the group of countries leading the process met together with the World Bank, the IMF and the EU in Brussels to discuss macroeconomic policies to help integrate Kosovo into the region and, ultimately, into the EU. They decided upon a macroeconomic policy that would include "a liberal trade and customs system, a stable currency, a functioning banking system, a regulatory framework that would ensure property rights, and a sustainable budget for the provision of basic services" (Skendaj 2014a, 120).

UNMIK had to raise local revenues since the donors were not prepared to fully finance Kosovo's budget deficit. The problem was resolved in two ways: the Group of Eight, the World Bank and the IMF decided to fund a higher budget deficit for a limited time, while the EU would take responsibility for rapidly developing the customs service along the borders with Kosovo's neighbours (ibid.). The core idea behind it is to increase revenue levels by making it "rational for business entrepreneurs to pay taxes instead of avoiding them" (Blair et al. 2005, 219).

Moreover, by establishing a stable flow of domestic revenue to fund public services UNMIK also planned to undermine the grey and black economy that had emerged during the war and had created links among various criminal networks in the region (concerning illegal trade with cigarettes, fuel, arms, human trafficking). By providing basic services and public goods, it was intended to reduce the population's reliance on such networks (Skendaj 2014a, 120–121).

Both the UN and EU discussed early on how to pursue the goal of establishing a functioning customs service. The first idea was to set up a similar system as for UNMIK's international police and to bring foreign experts into Kosovo. However, a British customs director from the European Commission managed to deter UNMIK officials from this policy—his experience in Bosnia and Herzegovina after 1995 and in Albania after the state collapsed in 1997 led him to recommend that UNMIK use local staff. The problem was that, during the Yugoslav period, due to its non-republic status Kosovo did not have its own customs service, even though quite a few officials from Kosovo worked in the Federal Yugoslav Customs Service (Skendaj 2014a, 121).

The EU hired 37 of those officials, with the service gradually expanding the number of workers over the years. Initially there was only one international officer for customs in Kosovo—the director-general. With the passing of time, their number rose from three to four international customs officers holding the highest positions. Their tasks were first and foremost to insulate the customs service from political influence and interference. They also enjoyed direct access to the Office of the SRSG, enabling them to dictate policies in their field without fear of an UNSC veto (Skendaj 2014a, 121–123).

Interestingly, Paul Acda (in Skendaj 2014a, 122–123), the first international customs officer in Kosovo of British origin, states the international community had no idea of how to establish a customs service from scratch. Hence, as a precedent for Kosovo Acda took the example of the establishment and development of the customs service in the Russian Federation. That body was formed after dissolution of the USSR (before the Soviet Union's collapse, its customs service was insignificant: it employed less than 3000 people as the Soviet Union did not engage in free trade, hence only focused on its own goods and people who went abroad, disregarding those flowing into the country). The borders were managed by the KGB. When the USSR fell apart, the customs service had to be established despite the small revenues the country could offer to future officials (they had to increase their number six-fold).

The solution adopted by the Russian Federation at the beginning of the 1990s was to recruit young people. The most suitable were aged around 18 years old, not holding university degrees. These young people were then given a chance to enrol in universities and academies for five years to graduate from economics, law, finance etc. In this way, they were 'made' customs officers immediately after school. These students were told they were part of an elite group of young people given college education to lead and manage an important component of the Russian Federation's governance (ibid.). As Skendaj (2014a, 123) puts it: "the Russian officers started doing work at the age of 22, sharing the idea that they were doing something important for their nation".

A similar approach, albeit not on such a big scale, was followed in Kosovo. This strategy also brought good results in terms of including ethnic minorities in the emerging institutions of the Kosovar government (with an exception of the Kosovo Serbs who were understandably not interested in joining). As most of the other-than-Serb minorities living in Kosovo did not have a high education, those leading this process decided to lower the entry bar in some regions (only secondary education was required).[9] What is more, women also started to join the ranks in

---

[9]Today, the ethnical division numbers are estimated at 85 to 90% of the population being Albanian, between 6 and 10% Serbs, 3–4% Bosnian, 1–2% Turks, Roma, Ashkali and Egyptians together comprising 2–3% of the population, and Gorani representing between 0.5 to 1% of the population. When taking the median into account, we can conclude that the ethnic composition of Kosovo Customs even today relatively fairly represents the ethnic composition of the population, especially when it comes to Albanian and Serbian representatives. The figures are slightly

greater numbers. This is not surprising given that unemployment has always been high in Kosovo (Skendaj 2014a, 123–124).

4.3.2 Customs in the EULEX Period

By April 2007, all customs operations were being run by local officials. The EU was always involved through both UNMIK and bilaterally. The Kosovo Customs has benefited from developmental assistance programmes such as IPA, twinning programmes and other EU-led initiatives. The programme reports from the period before EULEX's deployment in 2008 are positive. The 2007 Kosovo progress report noted good overall progress in the field of customs. It acknowledges that the adoption of the Kosovo Customs Code in March 2004 was broadly compliant with the EU legislation. It further noted the system for directly connecting and monitoring all border points had been operational since March 2007 (EULEX Progress Report 2007).

Serious efforts have also been made to ensure greater public confidence in Customs and enable the reporting of possible corruption (EULEX Programme Report 2007). Especially the former—corruption and protection of the customs service from political influences—was the main approach the international actors used to build up this sector in the years after the war in Kosovo. As Skendaj (2014b, 471) states, "from early on, one key task of the international administrator was to prevent political interference from the Kosovo self-government institutions or UNMIK" and to successfully import the EU's rules and institutional mechanisms to penalise corruption in the customs service.

Due to the nature of the customs service, it holds "high potential for corruption since it processes taxes at the border and its officials have strong incentives to misrepresent the goods in exchange for a large bribe" (Skendaj 2014b, 468). The customs bureaucracy could therefore be one of the most corrupt and least effective institutions around the world; this holds true for many post-conflict societies. However, as our interviewees argue, the internal institutional mechanisms put in place in Kosovo have worked relatively well to control and prevent corruption.

Complaints about possible misconduct by customs officers have been examined. Individuals found guilty of abusing their positions have been punished. In UNMIK's initial years, many Kosovo Albanian officers were removed from the service by this mechanism. Afterwards, despite the considerable potential for corrupt behaviour the Kosovo customs service has been quite successful in disciplining such misconduct, especially compared to other customs services in other countries in the region (ibid.).

---

underrepresented in the case of the Roma/Ashkali/Egyptian minorities and the Bosnian minority, while Turks are slightly overrepresented. It is also clear from the graphs presented above that the numbers of police employees have changed greatly in the last 8 years, especially in regard to Serb minority—whose numbers have almost doubled since 2012.

When EULEX took over, it first and foremost had to ensure the continuation of the managerial capabilities so as to limit any political influence on the customs service. This was done by the previously mentioned international officers who could be found on the outside of the 'patronage networks' that could give jobs in exchange for personal loyalty. Therefore, they were able to evaluate the knowledge of selected locals and complete the recruitment process for top positions in the customs service. The technical assistance service ensured the most capable candidates with the best managerial skills at the time were chosen (Skendaj 2014a, 129–130).

Immediately after independence, the Kosovo government tried to politicise the customs service by firing its director, but was forced to reinstate him after immense pressure from the EU and the USA. In 2010, a similar attempt was again made; once more EULEX did not hesitate to intervene and took measures to oppose this act. The attempts to politicise customs (as well as police) undermined the authority and impartiality of these institutions (ibid.).

Today Kosovo continues to rely economically to a great extent on the collection of customs revenues arising from international trade. The customs service raises approximately 70% of Kosovo's state revenues every year (Compact progress report 2015). Customs has ensured that Kosovo's self-government budget has been fully financed by domestic sources already since 2003 (Skendaj 2014b, 467). Hence, it is considered one of the most crucial sectors in Kosovo.[10]

4.3.3   EULEX's Normative Power in the Customs Sector

It is clear the EU was ready to play its role as a normative actor in the customs sector. After 1999, it took the initiative in the fourth pillar of UNMIK—overseeing customs—and saw it as its obligation to also contribute to peace in Kosovo in this way. At the same time, contributing to the growth of general revenues by collecting taxes from international trade worked well for the economic logic underlying the EU's peacebuilding efforts: aiming to successfully engage the state to build a strong institution for collecting revenue.

Before 2008, the EU had achieved four (out of the five) criteria needed for it to be perceived as a normative actor. First, it built up its normative identity in interaction with others; it has successfully overtaken the fourth UNMIK pillar (reconstruction and economic development). Moreover, the EU used normative means in its activity: regulations, setting an example in this area and its customs blueprints (guidelines for strengthening the customs sector), which "allowed for overall coherence in terms of formal rules as well as flexibility for its field operations" (Skendaj 2014b, 471).

---

[10]The studies of earlier European and American state-building processes indicate that revenue extraction was crucial for ensuring the state's longevity and the accountability of states to their citizens (Skendaj 2014a, 182).

Customs officers also received both formal and on-the-job training as part of preparing for their position. Recruits had to go through eight weeks of formal training after which there was a six-month probation period. In any of these stages, a recruit could lose their position if they did not meet the expected performance behaviour or engaged in corrupt activity. The customs service also provided for clear evaluation policies—performance indicators and relevant promotion policies within a definite hierarchy (Skendaj 2014b, 472).

In terms of normative behaviour, once again the EU not only acted according to its own values (tax collection and revenue from international trade is extremely important for the EU), but also imported this behaviour directly through the mentioned blueprints and regulations. In terms of the normative ends achieved— correcting attitudes in a post-conflict society the EU wished to influence—it is, as our interviewees believe, clear that in this period the EU was successful in penalising corrupt behaviour and political influences that could affect the revenue collected through the customs service.

What can we say about the EU's 'others-empowering' normative interests in the case of EULEX's customs service mandate? It is evident that if the EU wanted to stabilise Kosovo, it had to work on improving the economic situation in the country which, as illustrated, largely occurred via the customs service. EULEX has supported structural changes in Kosovo Customs that led to real progress such as 5% increase in customs revenue collection and a 500% rise in the sum of undeclared cash seized at Pristina airport customs. The mission has supported Kosovo Customs in implementing full customs controls and collecting associated revenues and taxes at the crossing points in the north of Kosovo (EULEX 2016a).

Following the EU-facilitated Dialogue between Kosovo and Serbia, the Development Fund for Northern Kosovo municipalities was established in 2013. The fund is made up of revenues collected at the crossing points of "Gate 1" (Jarinje) and "Gate 31" (Brnjak) and distributed to development projects in Northern Kosovo. The Fund is managed by a management board composed of the EUSR in Kosovo as the Chair, the Kosovo Minister of Finance on behalf of the Kosovar authorities, and a representative of the Serb community in the four municipalities (Peci 2013).

While several Kosovo Albanian opposition politicians remain critical of this EU initiative due to the presumed creation of a parallel budget for Serbian municipalities that could lead to the further loss of control over the north of Kosovo, the initiative's main goal is to foster the social and economic development of people in the northern municipalities, to fight against instability and poverty and, ultimately, to reduce the threat of home-grown radicalism, which could also arise from the dire economic situation (ibid.). By 1 March 2016, the Fund had collected more than EUR 8.3 million. As at that date, the management board had approved 13 different projects involving a total of EUR 6.4 million (European Union Office in Kosovo 2017).

Moreover, several other activities are performed through EULEX that in a way also help the EU keep the Union safe. Several EU actions have been dedicated to increase the capacity of Kosovo customs, including twinning in the field of

Integrated Border Management and the fight against drug trafficking, as well as in the area of fighting organised crime (European Commission 2015). Tzifakis (2013) adds that EULEX helped Kosovo Customs adopt and further develop the Kosovo Customs Code in line with European standards, and especially to realise some progress in developing its cooperation and information sharing with other Kosovo law-enforcement agencies.

Another recent challenge of great relevance is the control of irregular migration across Kosovo's borders. During the increased influx of migrants toward the EU in 2015, but also before then, an extensive spike in irregular migration from Kosovo to EU countries was noted. The EU-sponsored dialogue with Serbia on irregular migration led to closer cooperation with Belgrade in this area (Kosovo Report 2015) and the Kosovo Border Police has, hand in hand with Kosovo customs, taken actions to address this pressing issue.

As shown in a 2016 Report of the EUHR for the UNSG on EULEX's activities in Kosovo, the mission held an advisory and support role for the Kosovo border police and customs on the country's preparedness in the event of a considerable influx of migrants.[11] However, long-term and comprehensive policies to prevent any further spikes in irregular migration must still be considered and addressed.[12]

While those challenges do not directly fall within the scope of the mission's original mandate, they form constitutive parts of the broader security environment and hold direct and indirect implications for the mission's operational work (Interview 20 2016r). Changes should be first implemented at the strategic level and then all the way down to the tactical level, and should be accompanied with adequate financial adaptations to support the directions set (top-down approach).

It should be noted that the past attempts to prioritise specific issues following the "bottom-up approach" have been identified as only partly successful (Interview 8 2016g). Due to its rigid and lengthy planning process, the mission's flexibility is limited. It usually takes 1 year to 1.5 years for the mission to change its direction and operational focus, which is not suitable if it is to address such imminent challenges.

We may therefore conclude there are many 'self-empowering' interests invested in improving the customs service in Kosovo. By improving the customs service in Kosovo, the EU becomes safer in terms of reducing the chance of having a 'social time bomb' exploding on its doorstep. In addition, it can cooperate with capable local authorities in terms of preventing money laundering, organised crime, human trafficking and, more recently, irregular migration threats from the south.

Capussela (2015, 116) states that organised crime and threats such as terrorism through a lack of control over irregular migration pose obvious direct risks for Europe. On the other hand, corruption and economic crime are included in the

---

[11]Report of the Secretary-General on the United Nations Interim Administration Mission in Kosovo, 2016, S/2016/407. http://www.un.org/en/ga/search/view_doc.asp?symbol=S/2016/407

[12]Measures are also needed to tackle the underlying causes of emigration, in particular high unemployment, especially among young people.

mandate because corruption and related economic crime are both a (proximate) cause of state fragility and the necessary companions of organized crime. Since Kosovo is losing its 'peacebuilding momentum', some of the solutions (such as increased flexibility of the mission in order for the mandate to adapt to more pressing threats) are still not being considered by the EU member states.

Achievements in border control and state security—normative ends?
However, the EU was able to achieve many peacebuilding normative ends in the case of the customs service. The 2009 EULEX Programme Report noted that Kosovo customs officials were quite well trained to perform their basic duties, that the government strategy on integrated border management had been adopted, and that operational plans had been developed. The main challenges then identified were the lack of adequate equipment and facilities, staff shortages, poor communication and the particularly low level of intelligence exchanged between customs, the Kosovo Police and other law-enforcement agencies. The report also noted that overall the customs legislation is insufficient and there is a strong need for advanced and "tailor-made" trainings etc. (EULEX 2009 Programme Report).

If we compare the state of affairs in customs half a decade later (Compact Progress Report 2015), we can observe an improvement in the internal restructuring of Kosovo Customs and improved recruitment; yet staff shortages remain a challenge. A new 'paperless customs system' has been introduced which, in addition to facilitating trade, responded to and addressed alleged corrupt practices.

An important development is the construction of permanent border crossing points between Kosovo and Serbia. An agreement on Integrated Border Management between Kosovo and Serbia was reached in December 2011, and the technical protocol was initiated in 2012. It was immediately signed by Kosovo, whereas the Serbian side stalled signing it by 7 months (European External Action Service 2014, 21). The process was later followed by an agreement on an Action Plan which, together with the Technical Protocol, laid down two phases of integrating the border management.

The first phase included the establishment of temporary buildings, followed by building permanent premises in line with EU standards in the second phase. The parties agreed to establish six border crossing points, three of which were located in Kosovo and the other three of them in Serbia (Interview 13 2016k). Yet the implementation process did not run smoothly, as it was marred by different incidents resulting from counterreactions, including the burning and damaging of facilities at the border crossing points at Brnjak and Jarinje in 2011, while shots were fired at local and KFOR personnel at both border crossing points.

Six months later, attacks were also reported in Zvečan/Zveçan, injuring German troops (European External Action Service 2014, 21). According to one interview, full presence and functionality at the Brnjak and Jarinje border crossing points were restored in 2013 with the Operational Plan of EULEX. The plan was drafted by Kosovo Customs and took account of all agreements made during the meetings in Brussels, as well as the Kosovo legislation and conclusions from the technical negotiations on Integrated Border Management. The clearance of all goods and collection of customs duties, excise duties and VAT commenced at the Jarinje and Brnjak border crossing points on 14 December 2013 as a result of the conclusions negotiated in Brussels (Interview 21 2016s).

With regard to regular border patrols on the so-called green border, KFOR troops in particular noted that EULEX does not have sufficient capabilities and manpower to effectively execute the border control tasks, placing an extra burden on KFOR (Interview 17 2016o). Due to the lack of border control capabilities, certain parts of the green border remain exposed and vulnerable; one of the main problems in the area is illegal logging. Such criticism applies most strongly to the north of Kosovo where for security and political reasons EULEX staff only have a limited capability to contribute to border control, although the situation has improved significantly in the last couple of years (Interview 19 2016q). On the other hand, the EU's wider engagement in border control, especially the mentioned agreement on Integrated Border Management for crossing points, has brought substantive progress to the normalisation of border management with Serbia (Interview 13 2016k).

While certain interviews indicate the green border remains a key challenge not sufficiently addressed by Kosovo Customs and EULEX, the official reports do suggest improvements. EULEX facilitates meetings with KFOR, while organising joint trainings with the Kosovo Border Police and Kosovo Customs aimed at developing an operational plan for these "green border patrols" (Compact Progress Report 2015).

The mission also has an important role in facilitating interagency meetings among relevant Kosovar stakeholders in border management (e.g. customs, police, food and veterinary agency, tax office etc.). These meetings are held on both the national level and in coordination with the Serbian counterparts (Interview 11 2016j). Specifically, within customs joint meetings on the regional level between Serbian and Kosovo customs staff have taken place every two months (Interview 14 2016l). EULEX has therefore helped normalise the relations between Kosovo and Serbia by taking steps in the direction of bringing representatives from both sides to the table, establishing the exchange of information, along with a certain degree of coordination and cooperation (Interview 15 2016m).

With the goal to achieve higher interoperability and efficiency in border management, EULEX supported the establishment of the National Centre for Border Management. The centre facilitates the collection, analysis and dissemination of information, and supports cross-border and regional cooperation. The centre is also one of the most important benchmarks achieved on the Kosovo roadmap for visa liberalisation (EULEX 2016b).

Normative identity tested
One can find different evaluations of customs and, interestingly, the poor public evaluations of customs as being one of the most corrupt governmental services have continued despite the relatively small number of cases brought to court (European

Court of Auditors 2012). The UN Development Programme (UNDP) Public Pulse Report 2015 shows that 32.3% of respondents identified Customs as one of the most corrupt government agencies in Kosovo (UNDP 2016). This public perception of corruption in Kosovo Customs remains a *perceived* challenge, endangering the EU's image as a normative actor in this field. It is necessary to increase public confidence in the national institutions to assist the EU in its goal of being perceived as a force for good in the country.

However, Skendaj (2014a, 109) explains this deviation from the otherwise well-perceived Customs' success and notes that "when asked about their sources for evaluating the extent of the corruption, 46% of the respondents claimed it was based on the media, and only 10% claimed they had a personal experience with the corruption". Skendaj (2014b, 469) also notes that the "customs service is constantly ranked as the most responsive bureaucracy in Kosovo by various assessments, both national and international. According to the responsiveness to public requests assessments by the Youth Initiative for Human Rights, the customs service received the maximum possible rating of 100% and stood out high above all other local institutions" since it responded to all public requests for information demanded by this non-governmental organisation.

In concluding this assessment, we evaluate the EU's impact on Kosovo Customs as mostly positive. The European Court of Auditors' report (2012) viewed the EU's assistance as largely having achieving its objectives of building the capacity of Kosovo Customs, leading to increased revenue collection, improvement in the fight against money laundering, a contribution to reforming the customs regulations and their implementation.

Similarly, according to the European Commission's Kosovo 2015 Report, the country is moderately prepared in the area of customs, and while its customs legislation is largely compliant with the EUs' customs code, Kosovo is advised to implement customs legislation in line with EU practices (European Commission 2015, 40). The report states that the Kosovo Customs operates throughout Kosovo, although only to a limited extent in the north. This has improved in the last years. Accordingly, we may conclude that the EU has succeeded in attaining its goal of transferring EU best practices to Kosovo Customs and to some extent in providing sufficient technical capabilities to enforce them.

On the other hand, certain shortcomings must still be addressed. According to the mission statement, EULEX shall assist the Kosovo institutions in their progress towards sustainability and accountability and in further developing and strengthening multi-ethnic police and customs service, ensuring that these institutions are free from political interference and adhering to internationally recognised standards and European best practices (Declaration on the European Union Rule of Law Mission in Kosovo 2008). Specific mission tasks in relation to Kosovo Customs are defined to help ensure that all Kosovo rule-of-law services, including the customs service, are free from political interference; contribute to the fight against corruption, fraud and financial crime; make sure that all its activities respect international standards concerning human rights and gender mainstreaming etc. (ibid.).

Therefore, EULEX's main task in the future is, as mentioned, to ensure that customs remains (or become even more) politics-free in the future. This would make sure the service continues on a professional basis and show the EU is indeed basing its normative behaviour in the country on its own values—impartiality, anti-corruption, as well as strong democratic institutions in which minorities and social groups are equally represented. Moreover, EU member states are expected to remain on their toes about Kosovo's future and pay attention to threats like migration, radicalism, terrorism and home-grown foreign fighters. A true normative actor should provide long-term solutions to these imminent threats and challenges, although EU member states might already be losing their interest in providing funding and real solutions for this conflict-torn country.

References

Aliu, L. (2017). Waiting on the judges from the north. Retrieved January 8, 2018, from http://kosovotwopointzero.com/en/ne-pritje-te-gjykatesve-nga-veriu/.

B92. (2008). EU to postpone sending mission to Kosovo. Retrieved November 16, 2017, from https://web.archive.org/web/20110606231841/http://www.b92.net/eng/news/politics-article.php?yyyy=2008&mm=01&dd=15&nav_id=46936.

Blair, S. A., Eyre, D., Salome, B., & Wasserstrom, J. (2005). Forging a viable peace: Developing a legitimate political economy. In J. Covey, M. J. Dziedzic, & L. R. Hawley (Eds.), *The quest for viable peace: International intervention and strategies for conflict transformation.* Washington, D.C: United States Institute of Peace Press.

Bonefeld, W. (2012). Freedom and the strong state: On German Ordoliberalism. *New Political Economy, 17* (5), 633–656.

Borgh, C. van der. (2012). Resisting international state building in Kosovo. *Problems of the Post-Communism, 59*(2), 31–42.

Boštjančič Pulko, I., & Pejič, N. (2016). Drawing lessons learnt on operational capabilities of EU's CSDP missions in Kosovo and Bosnia and Herzegovina. *European Perspectives, 8*(1), 109–129.

Capussela, A. L. (2015). *State-building in Kosovo: Democracy, corruption and the EU in the Balkans.* London: I.B. Tauris & Co Ltd.

Cerone, J., & Baldwin, C. (2003). Explaining and evaluating the UNMIK court system. Retrieved January 8, 2018, from https://ssrn.com/abstract=1647211.

Cierco, T., & Reis, L. (2014). EULEX's impact on the rule of law in Kosovo. *Revista de Ciencia Politica, 33*(3), 645–663.

Cigler, M. (2017). Speech at the Balkan SAYS conference 2017 in Kranjska Gora on 11 October 2017.

Compact progress report. (2015). Assessing progress between July 2014–July 2015. Retrieved January 8, 2018, from http://www.eulex-kosovo.eu/eul/repository/docs/CPReport_2N.pdf.

Council Decision 2014/349 CFSP of 12 June 2014 amending Joint Action 2008/124/CFSP on the European Union Rule of Law Mission in Kosovo, 2014. Retrieved February 4, 2017, from http://eur-lex.europa.eu/legal-content/EN/TXT/PDF/?uri=CELEX:32014D0349&from=EN.

Council Joint Action. (2008a). 2008/123/CFSP of 4 February 2008 appointing a European Union Special Representative in Kosovo, Official Journal L 42/88, 16 February 2008. Retrieved January 6, 2018, from http://eur-lex.europa.eu/legal-content/EN/TXT/?uri=CELEX%3A32008E0123.

Council Joint Action. (2008b). 2008/124/CFSP of 4 February 2008 on the European Union Rule of Law Mission in Kosovo, EULEX Kosovo, Official Journal L 42/92, 16 February 2008. Retrieved January 8, 2018, from http://www.eulex-kosovo.eu/eul/repository/docs/WEJointActionEULEX_EN.pdf.

Council of the European Union. (2008b). Javier Solana, EU high representative for the CFSP, announces the start of EULEX Kosovo (S400/08). Retrieved January 8, 2017, from http://www.consilium.europa.eu/uedocs/cms_Data/docs/pressdata/en/declarations104524.pdf.

De Wet, Erika. (2009). The governance of Kosovo: security council resolution 1244 and the establishment and functioning of EULEX. *The American Journal of International Law, 103* (84), 83–96.

Eckhard, S. (2016). *International assistance to police reform: Managing peacebuilding.* London: Palgrave Macmillan.

EEAS. (2016). Release of the upgraded Goalkeeper/Schoolmaster website (press release). Retrieved December 21, 2017, from https://eeas.europa.eu/headquarters/headQuarters-homepage/9117/release-upgraded-goalkeeperschoolmaster-website_en.

Ejdus, F. (2017). The EU rule of law mission in Kosovo: Lessons for the EU. Retrieved January 8, 2018, from https://europeanwesternbalkans.com/2017/10/09/bsf-eu-rule-law-mission-kosovo-lessons-eu/.

Ejdus, F., & Juncos A. E. (2017). Reclaiming the local in EU peacebuilding: Effectiveness, ownership, and resistance. *Contemporary Security Policy,* 1–24.

EULEX Progress Report. (2007). Kosovo under UNSCR 1244, 2007 progress report. Retrieved December 11, 2017, from http://eeas.europa.eu/delegations/kosovo/documents/eu_kosovo/2007_commission_progress_report_kosovo_en.pdf.

EULEX. (2009). EULEX programme report 2009. Prishtina: European Union rule of law mission (EULEX) in Kosovo. Retrieved January 8, 2018, from http://www.eulex-kosovo.eu/eul/repository/docs/EPR_2009_2.pdf.

EULEX. (2010). EULEX programme report 2010: Building sustainable change together. Prishtina: European Union rule of law mission (EULEX) in Kosovo. Retrieved January 8, 2018, from http://www.eulex-kosovo.eu/eul/repository/docs/EPR_2010_2.pdf.

EULEX. (2016a) *EULEX implements its mandate through four operational objectives.* Retrieved December 1, 2017, from http://www.eulex-kosovo.eu/?page=2,44.

EULEX. (2016b). EULEX supports the establishment of national centre for border management. Retrieved December 17, 2017, from http://www.eulex-kosovo.eu/?page=2,27,360.

EULEX. (2016c). Executive division. Retrieved January 8, 2018, from http://www.eulex-kosovo.eu/?page=2,2.

European Commission. (2012). Commission communication on a feasibility study for a stabilisation and association Agreement between the European Union and Kosovo. Retrieved July 31, 2017, from https://ec.europa.eu/neighbourhood-enlargement/sites/near/files/pdf/key_documents/2012/package/ks_analytical_2012_en.pdf.

European Commission. (2015). Joint communication to the european parliament and the council: Capacity building in support of security and development—enabling partners to prevent and manage crises. Retrieved July 30, 2017, from http://eur-lex.europa.eu/legal-content/EN/TXT/PDF/?uri=CELEX:52015JC0017&from=EN.

European Court of Auditors. (2012). European Union assistance to Kosovo related to the rule of law. Special Report no. 18. Retrieved August 24, 2017, from http://www.eca.europa.eu/Lists/ECADocuments/SR12_18/SR12_18_EN.PDF.

European External Action Service. (2014). State of play in implementation of the brussels agreement—report submitted to the European Union by the government of the Republic of Kosova. Retrieved November 10, 2017, from http://www.kryeministriks.net/repository/docs/Kosovo_Report_on_implementation_state_of_play_of_the_Brussels_Agreements_160114-signed.pdf.

European Union External Action (2015). *Short history of EULEX.* Retrieved February 4, 2016, from http://www.eulex-kosovo.eu/?page=2,44,197.

European Union office in Kosovo. (2017). Development fund. Retrieved November 8, 2017, from http://eeas.europa.eu/delegations/kosovo/eu_kosovo/development_fund/index_en.htm.

External Relations Council. (2008). External Relations Council meeting in Brussels, 18 February 2008, 6496/08 (Presse 41).

Greiçevci, L. (2011). EU actorness in international affairs: The case of EULEX mission in Kosovo. *Perspectives on European Politics and Society, 12*(3), 283–303. Retrieved January 29, 2018, from http://www.tandfonline.com/doi/abs/10.1080/15705854.2011.596307.

Grevi, G. (2009). The EU rule-of-law mission in Kosovo. In G. Grevi, D. Helly, & D. Keohane (Eds.), *European Security and Defense Policy: The first ten years (1999–2009)* (pp. 353–368). Paris: The European Union Institute for Security Studies.

Grilj, B., & Zupančič, R. (2016). Assessing the planning and the implementation of the law missions: Case study of EULEX Kosovo. *European Perspectives, 8*(2), 63–86.

Haug, H. K. (2015). Gender equality and inequality in Kosovo. In C. M. Hassenstab & S. P. Ramet (Eds.), *Gender (in)equality and gender politics in Southeastern Europe. Gender and politics*. London: Palgrave Macmillan.

IECEU. (2016b). *Deliverable 2.3 IECEU Study report of Kosovo and Bosnia and Herzegovina* (forthcoming). Retrieved January 8, 2018, from http://www.ieceu-project.com/?page_id=197.

Jacque, J. P. (2015). *Review of the EULEX Kosovo mission's implementation of the mandate with a particular focus on the handling of the recent allegations*. Report to the attention of the High Representative/Vice President of the European Commission. Retrieved January 8, 2018, from http://collections.internetmemory.org/haeu/content/20160313172652/http:/eeas.europa.eu/statements-eeas/docs/150331_jacque-report_en.pdf.

Kammel, A. (2011). Putting ideas into action: EU civilian crisis management in the Western Balkans. *Contemporary Security Policy, 32*(3), 625–643.

Kosovo Prosecutorial Council. (2017). Meeting of the Joint Rule of law Coordination Board held in Pristina. Retrieved December 7, 2017, from http://www.kpk-rks.org/en/single_lajmi/1618/u-mbajt-takimi-i-radhs-i-bordit-t-prbashkt-bashkrendues-pr-.

Kosovo Report. (2015). Kosovo 2015 report—commission staff working document. Retrieved November 8, 2017, from http://ec.europa.eu/enlargement/pdf/key_documents/2015/20151110_report_kosovo.pdf.

Kursani, S. (2013). A comprehensive analysis of EULEX. What next? Retrieved February 17, 2017, from http://www.kipred.org/en/news/A-COMPREHENSIVEANALYSIS-OF-EULEX-WHAT-NEXT-135.

Lixinski, L. (2013). *Intangible cultural heritage in international law*. Oxford: Oxford University Press.

Mac Ginty, R. (2017). The limits of technocracy and local encounters: The European Union and peacebuilding. *Contemporary Security Policy, 1*–14.

Mahr, E. (2017). Local contestation against the European Union Rule of Law Mission in Kosovo. *Contemporary Security Policy, 1*–23.

Malešič, M., & Juvan, J. (2015). Analiza operacij kriznega upravljanja EU. *Teorija in Praksa, 52* (5), 844–864.

Peci, E. (2013). Fund collects cash for north Kosovo Serbs. Retrieved January 8, 2018, from http://www.balkaninsight.com/en/article/kosovo-north-caught-between-financial-bloom-and-division.

Qehaja, F. (2017). *International or local ownership? Security sector development in post-independent Kosovo*. Washington D.C.: Westphalia Press.

Qehaja, F., & Prezelj, I. (2017). Issues of local ownership in Kosovo's security sector. *Southeast European and Black Sea Studies, 17*(3), 403–419.

Radin, A. (2014). Analysis of current events: "Towards the rule of law in Kosovo: EULEX should go". *Nationalities Papers, 42*(2), 181–194.

Report of the Secretary-General on the United Nations Interim Administration Mission in Kosovo S/2016/407. Retrieved December 20, 2017, from http://www.un.org/en/ga/search/view_doc.asp?symbol=S/2016/407.

Skendaj, E. (2014a). *Creating Kosovo: International oversight and the making of ethical institutions*. Ithaca, NY: Cornell University Press.

Skendaj, E. (2014b). International insulation from politics and the challenge of state building: learning from Kosovo. *Global Governance: A Review of Multilateralism and International Organizations, 20*(3), 459–481.

Spernbauer, M. (2010). *EU peacebuilding in Kosovo and Afghanistan: Legality and accountability*. Leiden: Brill.

Transparency International. (2016). Corruption Perception Index. Retrieved October 30, 2017, from https://www.transparency.org/news/feature/corruption_perceptions_index_2016.

Tzifakis, N. (2013). The European Union in Kosovo, reflecting on the credibility and efficiency deficit. *Problems of Post-Communism, 60*(1), 43–54.

UNDP. (2016). Making the labour market work for women and youth. http://hdr.undp.org/sites/default/files/human_development_report_2016.pdf. Accessed 25 December 2017.

Weller, M. (2009). *Contested statehood: Kosovo's struggle for independence*. New York: Kosovo University Press.

WOSCAP. (2017). EU peacebuilding capabilities in Kosovo after 2008: An analysis of EULEX and the EU-facilitated Belgrade-Prishtina Dialogue. Part A of Deliverable 3.1: Desk Review Case Studies. Retrieved November 16, 2017, from http://www.woscap.eu/documents/131298403/131299900/Kosovo+report_PU+%285%29.pdf/3f0fb0f7-e81c-4e42-bdee-c43efabfafed.

Yannis, A. (2004). The UN as government in Kosovo. *Global Governance, 10*(1), 67–81.

Zupančič, R. (2015). *Kosovo: laboratorij preprečevanja oboroženih konfliktov, pokonfliktne obnove in izgradnje države*. Brno: Vaclav Klemm in Plzen: Zapadočeska univerzita v Plzni.

Zupančič, R., Pejič, N., Grilj, B., & Peen Rodt, A. (2017). The European Union rule of law mission in Kosovo: an effective conflict prevention and peace-building mission? *Journal of Balkan and Near Eastern Studies*, 1–19. Retrieved January 29, 2018, from http://www.tandfonline.com/doi/full/10.1080/19448953.2017.1407539.

Zupančič, R., & Udovič, B. (2011). Lilliputian in a Goliath world: the preventive diplomacy of Slovenia in solving the question of Kosovo's independence. *Revista românæa de ştiinţe politice, 11*(2), 39–80.

Interviews

Interview 1. (2016a). Interview with EULEX official, Pristina, 8 March 2016.

Interview 2. (2016b). Interview with EULEX official, Pristina, 8 March 2016.

Interview 3. (2016c). Interview with Kosovo Ministry of Public Administration official, 7 March 2016.

Interview 4. (2016d). Interview with EU official, Brussels, 30 March 2016.

Interview 6. (2016e). Interview with KFOR official, Pristina, 7 March 2016.

Interview 7. (2016f). Interview with Kosovo NGO representative, 7 March 2016.

Interview 8. (2016g). Interview with EULEX official, Pristina, 8 March 2016.

Interview 9. (2016h). Interview with EULEX official, Pristina, 8 March 2016.

Interview 10. (2016i). Interview with EUSR official, Pristina, 10 March 2016.

Interview 11. (2016j). Interview with EULEX official, Pristina, 8 March 2016.

Interview 13. (2016k). Interview with Kosovo customs official, Pristina, 11 March 2016.

Interview 14. (2016l). Interview with EULEX official, Pristina, 9 March 2016.

Interview 15. (2016m). Interview with Kosovo police official, Pristina, 10 March 2016.

Interview 16. (2016n). Interview with EULEX official, Pristina, 11 March 2016.

Interview 17. (2016o). Interview with KFOR official, Pristina, 7 March 2016.

Interview 18. (2016p). Interview with Kosovo Ministry of European Integration official, Pristina, 10 March 2016.

Interview 19. (2016q). Interview with Kosovo NGO representative, Pristina, 11 March 2016.
Interview 20. (2016r). Interview with EULEX official, Pristina, 8 March 2016.
Interview 21. (2016s). Interview with Kosovo customs official, online, 9 and 20 July 2016.

Chapter 5
Conclusion

In the complex post-conflict environment Kosovo found itself in after the war ended in 1999, it is almost impossible to isolate the factors that supported or hindered the success of the peacebuilding efforts and to thus argue that the performance in peacebuilding can be ascribed to a single peacebuilding actor. In this monograph, we only looked at one 'face' of the EU's engagement in Kosovo—the European Rule of Law Mission in Kosovo, known as EULEX. Nevertheless, we located this CSDP mission within the framework of a wider conundrum of several international actors active in Kosovo (international organisations, non-governmental organisations, states etc.) that, while aiming to contribute to sustainable peace in the country by projecting 'good norms', are often driven by their own agendas, goals and internal institutional struggles, which might hinder the success of its peacebuilding endeavours.

Analysing the most ambitious civilian mission launched under the CSDP umbrella is not an easy task. The mission to this day remains a flagship of the EU CSDP; it is one of those EU engagements around the world used by several scholars, experts and ordinary citizens of Kosovo to evaluate the EU's power in international relations and the institution's ability to efficiently build sustainable peace in war-torn societies. Although this book was limited to scrutinising one CSDP mission only, the findings also hold policy relevance for other post-conflict environments. Namely, in many other post-conflict countries 'receiving' the peacebuilding efforts of international organisations and other actors, similar processes relevant to peacebuilding theory and practice have been underway.

Other findings important for studies of normative power and peacebuilding in post-conflict societies also stem from this research project. Thus, below we discuss the three distinct, mutually overlapping sets of findings. The first set touches on *the core analysis of this book* and *answers the main research questions*. The second section focuses on the *theoretical and policy-related implications of this research for both peacebuilding in Kosovo generally and the peacebuilding approach pursued by the EU*. The third, final part is *epistemological and methodological in*

R. Zupančič and N. Pejič, *Limits to the European Union's Normative Power in a Post-conflict Society*, SpringerBriefs in Population Studies, https://doi.org/10.1007/978-3-319-77824-2_5

character as it considers the validity and reliability of interview-based research in post-conflict societies.

EULEX as a way for the EU to project its normative power in Kosovo's customs, police and judiciary

This book's main theme explores the sort of normative power actor the EU wanted to become in its peacebuilding efforts in Kosovo through one of its most ambitious engagements abroad—the EULEX rule-of-law mission—as well as what kind of power the EU has actually exercised in this respect as perceived by local residents (a normative power or 'simply' a powerful actor that uses any means to achieve its aims?). Drawing from the general research question, the monograph tried to demonstrate the effects of the EU's attempt to normatively influence developments in this post-conflict society via EULEX, and here the research assessed whether it is prudent for the EU to try to act normatively within the peacebuilding domain—and to thus be eventually perceived by the local community as 'a force for good' (a normative power actor). Last but not least, the research evaluated EULEX's direct impact in the three core areas of its engagement: improving the functioning of Kosovo's police, customs and judiciary.

Beginning at the end: the research shows that EULEX's work has to some extent benefitted the targeted areas. Generally speaking, Kosovo's police and customs perform better today than they did prior to EULEX's engagement. While EULEX has helped to strengthen both the police and customs, several management and leadership challenges remain, including a certain level of identified political interference. Inter-organisational communication and cooperation, especially in the Kosovo Police–Kosovo Prosecutorial Office relationship remain challenging, as revealed in several EU reports. Next, the judiciary in Kosovo still struggles to deal with serious cases of corruption and organised crime, a fact that is a big disappointment for the Albanian, Serb and other ethnic communities in Kosovo, EULEX staff (local and international) and external observers alike.

Our research also shows that EULEX has positively contributed in several ways to build sustainable peace in Kosovo, particularly in law enforcement training and establishing dialogue between the EU and local authorities (although this might not be considered too great achievement given most local actors in Kosovo, both Albanian and Serb, are keen on cooperating with the EU). EULEX's contribution has also been observed indirectly, e.g. by facilitating the dialogue between Belgrade and Prishtina, since this EU mission provided a framework for the two sides to cooperate.

Further assistance is required in training on the use of sophisticated equipment and ensuring that Kosovo Customs is well equipped to perform its work, especially while the EU continues to provide the necessary means to establish permanent border crossing points between Kosovo and Serbia. Special attention is also needed when addressing the high levels of publicly perceived corruption inside Kosovo Customs. Efforts should be made to investigate what is driving the continuously poor evaluations and to improve the public's perception of Kosovo Customs. Finally, because it is highly likely that the stronger influx of irregular migration in the region will continue, EULEX will also have to assist its Kosovo partners in monitoring and controlling such migrant flows in the future.

On a less positive note, this civilian mission's legitimacy has been seriously eroded by the cases of corruption among EULEX staff and the criticism of its reluctance to prosecute political and economic elites allegedly involved in organised crime and corruption. In this respect, our research corresponds with several analyses conducted by other scholars (see Chap. 4 for details). Thus, it is no surprise that a significant majority of the Kosovar population and local institutions would prefer to see the termination and withdrawal of this mission.

Regarding the efficient use of resources needed to achieve the required level of functioning of Kosovo's customs, police and judiciary, the picture is also not promising. The majority of 'locals' and 'internationals' believe EULEX has spent significantly too many resources (financial, human, material etc.) for its relatively modest contribution to the rule of law and sustainable peace. Some authors like Capussela (2015) even claim notwithstanding this enormous investment—far bigger than in other countries in the region in which the EU is also engaged—the improved functioning of these three sectors has been too slow. He adds the EU's efforts to bolster the rule of law in Kosovo have mostly failed. This is consistent with World Bank (2014) worldwide governance indicators from 2014 showing that Kosovo continues to score lowest in the Western Balkan region for the rule of law.[1]

With regard to the normativity of EULEX's approach to Kosovar institutions, it is noted that the target institutions have benefited from EULEX's policy, which calls for a balance in the ethnic and gender composition of local law-enforcement institutions. The representation of Kosovo Serbs and other minorities within them reflects the actual composition of society relatively well, with some minor deviations. What remains a challenge is the relatively small number of female police and customs officers. Several structural and cultural factors might explain this.

Theoretical and policy implications of the research

In spite of almost two decades of engagement by the EU and other international actors, Kosovo remains a partly free and semi-consolidated authoritarian regime. This is not something a country that supposedly adheres to the rule of law can be proud of. However, certain progress has been made and should be acknowledged (Freedom House 2016). In addition, Kosovo remains economically one of the least developed countries in Europe, with widespread unemployment and inactivity, especially among women and youth, "which leaves an ample amount of human potential unused, misused or underused" (UNDP 2016). Hence, when discussing the theoretical and policy implications of this research, one should recall that EULEX is only one, albeit a very robust and resourceful, international actor

---

[1]On the percentile rank of the Rule of Law indicator—this indicates the rank of a country among all countries in the world, with 0 corresponding to the lowest rank and 100 corresponding to the highest—Kosovo ranks 37th. The higher the number, the better the rule-of-law rating. In comparison, Albania has a ranking of 41, Bosnia and Herzegovina 49, FYR Macedonia 57, Montenegro 61 and Serbia 50.

involved in peacebuilding in Kosovo. It is within this interplay of different actors, including local ones, that the (un)success of EULEX should be discussed.

Yet this does not imply that EULEX could not have performed better in several areas. Last but not least, before discussing the implications, one might also question the attempt to isolate the added value of EULEX's involvement in the rule-of-law reform and argue that certain achievements or failures have been the exclusive result of EULEX's work.

Neither EULEX nor any other international engagement in Kosovo has managed to change the fact that people in this former Yugoslav province—almost 20 years after the Serbs (the FRY) *de facto* lost power over Kosovo—still largely rely on particularistic networks to access resources for survival. Yet, it would be too much to expect this local characteristic, peculiar to several post-conflict societies, can be effectively reversed by a single actor. As rightly argued by Skendaj (2014, 181), every war produces economic scarcity, insecurity and generalised distrust, whereby relying on local components often literally amounts to 'who you know' and 'who can help you' to provide basic needs that in more developed parts of the world are typically addressed by more or less efficient state administrations.

What does this mean in practice? In everyday life, which may still be improved in the direction of a modern state (supposedly always working for the greater equality and well-being of its citizens), could the rule of law have been better implemented? A wide network of people who benefit directly from engaging with international actors is developing around all the international organisations in Kosovo and foreign countries' embassies in this 'new-born country'.

By definition, this means some people are privileged over others and that meritocracy in, for example, the situation of getting a job is not always the case. This is yet another and hardly disputed characteristic of several post-conflict societies, not just Kosovo. The insistence of 'internationals', including those of EULEX, on an inclusive concept of peacebuilding has led to the scenario whereby some locals are invited to take part in projects solely to comply with donors' requirement to ensure the inclusion of locals.

The result in practice is that locals often agree to become subcontractors or collaborators of international organisations or foreign embassies in exchange for being awarded a project that directly benefits them in several ways (good financial remuneration, international travel, educational and training programmes funded by international actors, and other opportunities for internationalising the careers of 'chosen individuals'). The more resourceful the international organisation, the wider the network, with EULEX being an excellent case in point. Yet, faced with limited chances to lead a decent life, the locals cannot be blamed for taking advantage of such opportunities, at least not until they work legally and work to help stabilise the country.

What then are the lessons the EU and CSDP can draw from this? EULEX withdrew relatively early from its involvement in the customs reform. Given the above findings, some might propose that EULEX similarly consider withdrawing its involvement in the Kosovo Police because the continuation of its presence there is today questionable and adds to or exacerbates the locals' dependence on 'the internationals'. One exception might be the offices investigating serious and financial crime where the support and assistance of EULEX's top experts is still welcome.

If this is to happen, vast financial resources should be invested in the judiciary in an attempt to attract and engage the most competent foreign judges, prosecutors etc. to work for EULEX. If only the 'second best' international experts can be recruited, downsizing the mission might be a better option than having not so well qualified and trained experts among the EULEX staff. At this point, we already touched on the (supposed) equality of the EU member states which do not want to stay out of any important decisions and selections for CSDP positions. Further strengthening of Kosovo's judiciary could occur by properly addressing certain known cases of mismanagement or even illegal activities of Kosovo's elites, making further efforts to complete legal procedures within a reasonable time and by ensuring that the laws and EU best practices are fully applied in practice.

As noted specifically by the locals we interviewed, in one decade of its functioning EULEX has often regarded political stability within the country as sacrosanct, even if this has occasionally compromised the effectiveness of its operations. While looking at Kosovo in terms of preventing conflict or destabilisation, we may conclude that a relatively stable environment has been maintained. However, EULEX has only partly contributed to this 'stability' within the framework of the international actors' streamlined efforts. It should also be noted that these international efforts brought about greater stability for many people, but not all. We can nevertheless conclude, based on several interviews and observations by other authors, that this 'stability-above-all mantra' has sometimes been achieved by compromising the mission's fundamental objective of strengthening the rule of law in Kosovo.

Drawing from this, the following recommendation is offered: EULEX (or any other similar civilian CSDP mission) aiming to establish the rule of law in a post-conflict society should press the member states, which have the final say in CSDP decisions, to provide the wherewithal to fulfil the mission's mandate—even if, like in Kosovo, this may sometimes challenge the stability argument. In other words, it is not enough for EU member states to only provide funding for CSDP missions and operations, which is perhaps the easy part, and then claim the EU is wholeheartedly committed to building peace, while simultaneously questioning whether changes in a particular post-conflict society are occurring as fast as expected.

On the other hand, if the stability argument prevails at the expense of the unwavering implementation of reforms at the EU level it is better for the mission or operation's leadership to explicitly state the mandate's objectives cannot be met in such circumstances where full support is lacking. If this is the case, the CSDP mission or operation's leadership should require the mandate to be changed or suggest it be closed and withdrawn from the post-conflict society.

One of the fundamental challenges unlikely to be resolved in the near future is EULEX's relationship with the issue of Kosovo's recognition. As noted by experts, the EU has somehow adapted and learned to live with the fact that five EU member states do not recognise the statehood of Kosovo. Yet in this regard the EU should also question who the people leading the CSDP missions and operations are, and how does the local population perceive them.

Namely, in 2016 a senior diplomat from Greece was appointed the new head of EULEX. As noted by some interviewees, the majority population of Kosovo (Albanians) have a certain hesitation regarding the ambiguous position of non-recognising states that also participate in EULEX. Appointing as mission head a representative from Greece, a country that does not officially recognise Kosovo, might thus send the wrong political message even if they are competent for the job. Irrespective of the question of who the head of the mission is, they should not hesitate to criticise the country's institutions when required (even if in the local environment this might lead to accusations that EULEX is politically intervening in domestic politics).

A reconsideration of the duration of deployments, especially of judges and prosecutors, and improving the pre-deployment training in EU member states (especially the synchronisation and standardisation of trainings at EU level) would benefit the mission's operational capability and efficiency. Some interviewees also indicated that pre-deployment training of EULEX personnel should focus more on the culture, history and tradition of the environment of the mission since it not uncommon for someone who has been deployed to not have the necessary knowledge of these topics (insufficient cultural awareness). The challenge of providing deployed personnel with the required language skills—English and local languages—has existed ever since the CSDP's inception over a decade ago. It must be ensured—through different means and initiatives—that the understanding of Kosovo's challenges and the CSDP generally becomes more standardised for all staff coming to the mission.

EULEX has still not been entirely able to transfer European best practices to Kosovar institutions. It has been noted several times that understanding of what EU 'best practices' are is often not very clear among EULEX staff or their local counterparts. It is necessary for EULEX (and other CSDP civilian missions in general) to improve its effectiveness by recruiting more personnel on a contract rather than a secondment basis. Namely, contracted personnel usually have to pass tougher selection processes and be better than competing candidates such that it becomes more likely they are not lacking in education, competence or professionalism instead of primarily deploying personnel seconded from member states who do not necessarily go through competitive selection processes.

Additional efforts are especially needed in Northern Kosovo where EULEX still faces certain limits which, however, do not necessarily stem from EULEX's own failures but the political circumstances in the area. It is recommended that EULEX reach out to the Serbian population in the areas north of the Ibar River by showing that a better rule of law can also be partly achieved through EULEX's efforts at lower (non-political) levels and thereby demonstrate that EULEX is not an institution that does injustice to the Kosovo Serbs, as it has often been seen as doing, most notably in the verdict handed down to the local Kosovo Serb politician Oliver Ivanović.

As Kosovo is a sensitive political and security environment in which state institution officials remain hesitant to report the wrongdoings, criminal activities or political interference of their superiors, it is suggested that EULEX, or the EU Office in Kosovo, establish so-called protected channels to allow the reporting of cases of political interference, nepotism, political and criminal pressure etc., free of pressure 'from above'. Such pressure can take different forms, from less benign verbal accusations to more problematic varieties (e.g. the threat of losing one's job or even putting one's life at risk).

When CSDP military operations and civilian missions are inaugurated, the expectations of local communities, together with the ambitions of the EU and its member states, are usually high. This is understandable as they are often perceived as a remedy coming from the developed world to heal all the problems of a post-conflict society. Nevertheless, if from its inception the CSDP mission or operation does not aim to create a functioning state, or at least provide greater safety, security and a stronger rule of law such an endeavour is doomed to fail.

To do so, the political environment in the recipient country (with aspirations to improve the current state of affairs) must also be positive, allowing the mission or operation to conduct the tasks falling within its mandate. Here we mean that local security providers must be able to contain any disruption that might occur. However, these ambitious goals cannot be achieved solely through the efforts of a CSDP civilian mission or military operation. They require the strong political commitment of the main actors on the ground, local ownership, economic development, functioning state institutions, and the coordinated will and actions of other international actors involved in conflict-prevention and peacebuilding efforts in the post-conflict society.

CSDP engagements are primarily conceived as short-term conflict-prevention and crisis-management instruments. Yet, as saw in the analysis of EULEX, this mission has instead been used as long-term vehicle for post-conflict institution-building. Hence, one of the first discussions to be resolved at EU level is whether it is better for CSDP missions and operations to also be deployed in the long run. If the answer is positive, the EU's mandates and general approach should be adapted accordingly. This is particularly important in light of the new EU Global Strategy that states the CSDP ought become more responsive and set the EU's approach very ambitiously.

The lack of a clear end-state or exit strategy for CSDP missions and operations does not help prevent its engagements from being seen as 'eternal' and without 'feasible goals' by the local people who should benefit from the CSDP. This not only applies to EULEX, but to most other CSDP military operations and civilian missions.

The analysis showed that the EU's engagement cannot succeed without aligning the policies of the biggest international actors in the area. With regard to the Balkans, this in particular refers to the EU-USA alignment, while the alignment of CFSP/CSDP with the Russian Federation, like it or not, might be more challenging to achieve for reasons pertaining to the domain of the 'realpolitik' of influential states. If this strategic alignment of major actors is not ensured, all of the positive

contribution of the EU's engagement will remain limited to the tactical (low) level
(e.g. improving the work of the police in dealing with traffic safety and petty crime,
better performance of customs, certain administrative reforms...), while leaving the
main objectives of the missions or operations, which are strategic in nature, still to
be accomplished (e.g. fighting corruption and organised crime).

Even the substantial financial and human resources the EU spends on CSDP
engagements cannot help much in the absence of genuine aspirations of the EU
(and its member states) and the USA in Kosovo to go after those political and
economic elites allegedly involved in criminal activities. This would, however,
require renewed negotiations between the US government and the EU. If this level
of misaligned and unsynchronised approaches among influential international
actors persists, this will further justify the criticism that the EU (and the West
generally) should either strengthen the level of its intervention to ensure real change
in the post-conflict society or withdraw from the country.

On the other hand, it comes as no surprise that the EU and its member states, or
even the USA, generally do not become strategically and comprehensively involved
as the problems, at least for now, seem to be 'locally contained' from the security
aspect (and there are several other more pressing issues for both Washington and
Brussels than Kosovo). Political leaders of countries in the region, with rare
exceptions, generally enjoy the support of the West and are well aware of what the
EU, drowning in its own problems, wants: namely, that any problems affecting the
Balkans remain contained within the area without threatening to spill over, to avoid
any (further) flaring up of the wider region.

When grasping the EU's desire to become a 'force for good' instead of a
'regular' security actor, one that uses all means available to achieve the desired
outcome in peacebuilding, we must recall our theoretical predispositions: we have
analysed the EU based on a normative identity as a subjective term, created by the
EU itself and its interactions with others. In terms of the EU's normative identity, it
is very likely the EU structures wish for their peacebuilding efforts to be perceived
as being normative in nature.

However, this endeavour to be regarded as a genuine 'force for good' has
misaligned expectations from the outset. It has raised the local population's
expectations regarding EULEX's capabilities to tackle all of Kosovo's problems,
while then failing to deliver on its promises in the eyes of the same people—be it
regarding the corruption that still exists, the establishment of somehow functioning
relations between the Serbs and Kosovo Albanians, or tackling high-profile cases of
individuals allegedly involved in criminal activities.

This does not mean the EULEX personnel are not interested in fulfilling these
promises, but that 'Brussels is far away'. The EU member states actually dictate
policies, but cannot agree on the level of engagement or the country's status, which
often proves to counterproductive in the field. The EU (thus, EULEX) does not
have a strong stance on elite politicians regarding non-popular measures the mission tries to implement. Hence, the mission often sacrifices its position to maintain
somewhat stable relations between conflicting parties in the country. Local politicians of course directly blame the mission for the failures. If the EU can only

establish its normative identity in its interactions with others, this bad reputation therefore has a direct influence on the EU's status as a normative player.

Next, our theoretical framework presupposes that the EU as a normative actor should have the will to participate in foreign policy dimensions that are a statement of its values. Again, is the EU able to claim that EULEX not tackling high-profile cases is a value it wants to advocate as a peacebuilding actor? The EU also tolerates the local elites' misbehaviour within the country in exchange for relatively peaceful relations with the 'opposite' side—the consequence is ever more imposed compliance than a real 'normative pull factor'. This certainly holds implications for the EU's identity as an international peacebuilding and normative actor. Moreover, is the lack of the division of powers within the mission itself a reflection of Europe's democratic values? Are the goals it wants to achieve with, for example, management of the migration crisis in Kosovo, really others-empowering such that they reflect its true goals of peacebuilding?

However, and third, the EU should behave according to the established norms: the EU has indeed acted in line with international law, and acted according to the norms and principles set out, except concerning internal corruption within its own ranks, a fact that has strongly damaged its reputation.

Fourth, the EU should use normative means of power: to persuade by implying the future mutual gains. In its activities, the EU engages in operational civilian peacebuilding consisting of monitoring, training locals, enhancing capabilities—supporting EU practices and values, but the problem is how to precisely identify these values. On the other hand, the mission's executive mandate is hardly the means for normative power.

Finally, when assessing the EU as a normative power we must look at the 'good' outcomes. As mentioned in Chap. 2, there are not many real EU success stories here revealing the correcting of attitudes and re-creating behaviour (using the previous four criteria as a basis for this correction), to help replace conflict with peace in the future. It should address the underlying causes and provide alternative means to resolve conflict without violence or without allowing the triggers of conflict to intensify. In the absence of a functioning judiciary, this will hardly ever be the case.

Moreover, the lack of political solutions provided by EULEX has created a political vacuum for domestic actors reluctant to comply with the EU's conditions and contesting the EU's policy positions on normative grounds. Therefore, some of the EU's actions or disagreements are leading to non-normative outcomes (short rotations, leaving local elites in power, not prosecuting criminal activities, corruption within the mission and across the country) and taking advantage of them has become a political tool for domestic players. With this, the reluctant domestic actors have likely given rise to domestic sources of legitimacy—namely, their own—instead of the EU's.

Yet, the EU should be allowed to fail to some extent—it can be less successful in its efforts to use the EULEX mission as an instrument of its peacebuilding. It is indeed following a 'good path'; yet, it should continue to recruit truly motivated and experienced people and not compromise in this regard. The case of customs clearly shows the need to use the 'best you have', even if that means some form of 'brain drain' in the member states. However, this requires political will, something the member states lack in the case of Kosovo, especially after a decade of EULEX's functioning.

Internal political will, not only its external counterpart deriving from the international community, is therefore the foundation upon which an outside player might hope to achieve the end-goal of functioning state organs, like the judiciary. The judiciary requires sufficiently long deployments of the judges to at least complete the high-profile cases. It also requires enough 'guts' to prosecute those in the highest positions and prevent the country from descending into chaos. It requires enough patience and the will to defend the reforms that tackle corruption against the local criminal networks that are also politically influential. The EU should strongly unite in its future peacebuilding endeavours if it wishes to improve in this regard.

Epistemological/methodological challenges of (future) research in post-conflict societies

We conclude this monograph by addressing a few epistemological and methodological aspects of research issues in post-conflict societies. Most research looking at post-conflict societies, such as the one in this monograph, struggles with the question of how to distinguish accurate information from 'fake' information in an environment often unwelcoming of foreigners. The field of conflict prevention and peacebuilding—in which national and international actors do not always work hand-in-hand and at times even pursue different agendas—is an excellent case in point.

This is very important in cases where the researcher relies on interviews as the main fieldwork method (this is quite a realistic prospect given that most peace-building research projects use this method). Namely, when it comes to interviews it is quite difficult for the researcher to know how much truth is contained in the answers received; interviewees are 'only' human beings, with different underlying motivations and agendas. Thus, gaining the local population's trust and building a reputation for trustworthiness in a post-conflict society is likely to be one of the most challenging tasks for a non-local researcher.

What does the organisation of fieldwork in a post-conflict society—arranging interviews in most cases—usually look like in practice? The researcher typically makes a few interview arrangements in advance. As these arrangements in post-conflict societies are often prone to change, when 'in the field' the researcher knows that quite a few interviews might not be completed for one reason or another. In this respect, we should also mention 'the fluidity' of in-advance arrangements in South East Europe. Most researchers active there are well acquainted with the phrase, "*Zovi, kad dodješ, i dogovoričemo se*" (across the various languages in the region, this roughly translates to: 'Call once you arrive, and we will set the time'). The researcher must thus accept the reality that it is impossible to set things (too much) in advance from his comfortable chair back home, and be flexible upon arrival as much as possible. In practice, this sometimes means not conducting a single interview in a day—or completing dozens of them within a short period.

Things might become further complicated by the fact that conducting fieldwork in post-conflict societies has certain specifics and unwritten rules: it touches on sensitive issues and is thus challenging *per se*. This is amplified when one strives to conduct *academic research*—a type of research which is ambitious by definition as it aspires for theory-building. Many people in post-conflict societies are (unsurprisingly) quite hesitant to share sensitive information with others. This is particularly true of post-conflict societies where trauma and suspicion are often two omnipresent features of an individual's daily lived experience. Thus, how can a researcher—even an academic who supposedly adheres to the highest ethical standards—believe (and then claim in academic publications) the interviewees actually revealed the most crucial information? In other words, can the researcher thus argue that, given these costraints, the research has any significant scientific value?

Conducting interview-based research in a post-conflict society, in particular with people a researcher can relatively easily relate to, has certain advantages and also drawbacks (this book's authors share with the target population of this research the fact of having once belonged to the same country—Yugoslavia—and consider the cultural, linguistic and other ties as beneficial). Several interviewees feel more secure and are less reluctant to share their opinion with a researcher if feel a certain degree of connectedness with them.

After the initial fuzziness accompanying a researcher's arrival in a post-conflict environment, the researcher then slowly starts to get a grip and usually manages to conduct several interviews during quite a short stay. Then, all too soon the field trip is almost over and the researcher starts packing up whilst in the meantime saying good-byes and still trying to obtain a few more potential interviewees' telephone numbers or email addresses. These are people the researcher did not have time to meet or were simply not in the country during the visit.

After returning home, the researcher embarks on another challenging journey: the data analysis stage. By definition, this means complementing the existing knowledge (theory) with fresh data obtained 'on the ground', so as to build on that theory. Often being overwhelmed by the sheer amount of interviews and acquired information while 'in the field', it is usually in this phase—when the researcher is already well settled back home and is already analysing the data—that the question of 'are any pieces missing from this puzzle' appears.

Namely, the researcher can never be aware of 'the unknown unknowns'. Unfortunately, for the academic rigour and accuracy of findings (in other words, the researcher's career), there are many 'unknown unknowns' in post-conflict societies since these are places where so many international actors with often competing agendas fight for their (or their sponsors') 'right' or 'truth'. The picture is further blurred by the fact international actors involved in peacebuilding are staffed by experts with different personalities and different goals that do not necessarily support the building of sustainable peace; while a considerable share of such experts is undoubtedly motivated by the prospect of making the post-conflict society a better place to live in, not all of them primarily work with this noble goal in mind. Thus, how can a researcher argue that the findings are accurate—and develop theory on them—if the main pool of information is interviews?

Noting these difficulties, we continually question our own conclusions, or 'the truths' about the EU's power to project norms in post-conflict societies—this time focused on the case of EULEX in Kosovo. However, on balance we argue that one possible way for researchers of conflict prevention and peacebuilding to partly mitigate these problems is to *not* jump from one (post-conflict) society to another, from one conflict to another. Some sort of continuity is needed (although it is hard to judge how long this should be) so that local people in the post-conflict society realise the researcher is not working 'for someone' (many researchers, including one of this book's authors, were accused of being a spy).

If this can be achieved, it becomes clearer to the interviewees that the researcher is genuinely interested in 'their' post-conflict zone and that the answers they provide will in no case be used against the interviewee. Only then can the researcher eventually overcome the attitudes of distrust and suspicion within the local community, which hamper the possibility of doing high-quality research. (However, for different reasons some people in post-conflict societies never trust researchers.)

Building on our previous work in Kosovo, our local contacts, and also a certain level of credibility and trust we have perhaps acquired, we tried to address the research problem of this monograph also 'through' the lens of the locals. Our approach—like many others similar to it—may rightly be criticised for not fully conforming to the scientific principles of systematicity, replicability, reliability, and thus even for its validity. Yet, in the face of such critiques, we concur with scholars who argue that this ultimately boils down to a choice between the research taking place in the constrained conditions or the research not being conducted at all.

But, as alluded to above, we continue to wonder what is the actual use of assembling the pieces of information collected through this method. And we think we are aiming for this: not a giant leap, but maybe at least one small step forwards, building on earlier analyses of post-conflict societies, and challenging those written by scholars who rely on 'the armchair approach' in studies of post-conflict societies, those who never manage to experience the post-conflict environment in person.

When all is taken into account, we prefer to be physically present in a post-conflict society and conduct research from within than to look on from afar. With this concluding thought, we encourage scholars to not only keep visiting 'the field' and take enough time to collect sufficient interviews or questionnaires to meet the funder's requirements, but to stay in the post-conflict zone long enough and speak to as many people as possible, so as to make their own 'reality' of a particular post-conflict environment as accurate as possible. In any case, even this 'reality' will only end up on the bookshelf alongside several other *realities*.

References

Capussela, A. L. (2015). *State-building in Kosovo: Democracy, corruption and the EU in the Balkans*. London, New York: I.B. Tauris & Co Ltd.

Freedom House. (2016). *Freedom in the world 2016: Kosovo*. Retrieved November 21, 2017, from https://freedomhouse.org/report/freedom-world/2016/kosovo.

Skendaj, E. (2014). *Creating Kosovo: International oversight and the making of ethical institutions*. Ithaca, NY: Cornell University Press.

UNDP. (2016). *Making the labour market work for women and youth*. Retrieved December 25, 2017, from http://hdr.undp.org/sites/default/files/human_development_report_2016.pdf.

World Bank. (2014). *Worldwide Governance Indicators (WGI)*. Retrieved October 17, 2017, from http://info.worldbank.org/governance/wgi/index.aspx#reports.

Index

© The Editor(s) (if applicable) and The Author(s) 2018
R. Zupančič and N. Pejič, *Limits to the European Union's Normative Power in a Post-conflict Society*, SpringerBriefs in Population Studies,
https://doi.org/10.1007/978-3-319-77824-2